The Human Use
of Human Resources

McGraw-Hill Series in Management

Keith Davis and Fred Luthans,
Consulting Editors

The Human Use of Human Resources

Marvin Karlins
Professor of Management
University of South Florida

McGraw-Hill Book Company

New York St. Louis San Francisco Auckland Bogotá Hamburg
Johannesburg London Madrid Mexico Montreal New Delhi Panama
Paris São Paulo Singapore Sydney Tokyo Toronto

This book was set in Optima by Black Dot, Inc. (ECU).
The editors were Kathi A. Benson and Peggy Rehberger;
the production supervisor was Leroy A. Young.
The cover was designed by Charles A. Carson.
R. R. Donnelley & Sons Company was printer and binder.

THE HUMAN USE OF HUMAN RESOURCES

1 2 3 4 5 6 7 8 9 0 D O D O 8 9 8 7 6 5 4 3 2 1

Library of Congress Cataloging in Publication Data

Karlins, Marvin.
　　The human use of human resources.

　　Bibliography:　p.
　　Includes index.
　　1.　Personnel management.　I.　Title.
HF5549.K268　　　　658.3　　　　80-25582
ISBN 0-07-033298-3
ISBN 0-07-033297-5 (pbk.)

About the Author

MARVIN KARLINS, Professor of Management at the University of South Florida, received his Ph.D. from Princeton University. He is a prolific writer, having authored, coauthored, or edited fourteen books, including *Psychology and Society*, *The Other Way to Better College Grades*, and *Biofeedback*, and contributed numerous articles on the subjects of psychology and business to various professional journals. He has also been a consultant to a wide variety of businesses and governmental agencies, including the Peace Corps, the U.S. Air Force, State Farm Insurance, and Graham-Jones. He has served on the faculties of the University of Pittsburgh, City College of the City University of New York, and Southern Illinois University. In 1980 Professor Karlins was voted the outstanding teacher of the year in the School of Business at the University of South Florida.

In loving memory of Sheldon Weinberg,
a man who always practiced what this book preaches.

Contents

Preface

This book is about management and how *you* can become a better manager. It is also a book about psychology and how you can use it to accomplish both management *and* labor objectives on the job. And, finally, it is a book about the human use of human resources: an opportunity to transform the workplace into a *worth* place, a place where personal and economic growth can coexist.

A manager's job isn't easy. If 20 years as a consultant, psychologist, and professor of business has taught me anything, it is a profound sense of respect for the men and women who choose management as a career. Theirs is often a thankless job requiring unwavering dedication and boundless energy to deal with seemingly endless problems and crises. Yet, it is also an occupation of crucial importance, where a person *can* make a difference in the world. Management, in short, is "where the action is" . . . and that's where you probably want to be.

Although a manager's job is difficult, it can be mastered, and mastered well. The purpose of this book is to make you a better manager by showing you how to use human resources both effectively *and* humanely.

The first section of the text, "A Theoretical Orientation," will provide you with the philosophical and conceptual basis for human resource management. How to actually manage those resources effectively will be discussed in Section Two, "How to Be an Effective Human Resource Manager in the Real World." It is here that I will be teaching you the skills necessary to function successfully in the workplace—skills that can be learned, and have been, by thousands of individuals just like yourself. Finally, Section Three will be devoted to making *you* happier and more satisfied as a manager and is entitled, pointedly, "How to Succeed in Business without Really Dying."

There are today a growing number of individuals and corporations dedicated to making the job environment a better place to work. I salute their efforts. Yet, there is still a long way to go in the struggle for the human use of human resources. Being a manager in our changing world is a challenging mixture of opportunity and responsibility. I hope the information in this book will help make work more rewarding to both you and those you manage, and hasten the day when all labor and management can work together in a productive and personally satisfying manner.

Marvin Karlins

Acknowledgments

First and foremost, I recognize with gratitude the contributions of my students and colleagues to this effort. I would like to single out Dr. Keith Davis for his support and valuable contributions to the manuscript. Then, too, there is Dr. Harold Schroder, my doctoral adviser at Princeton University and associate at the University of South Florida School of Business. I acknowledge my continuing intellectual debt to him. Thanks are also due those authors whose published research reports I utilize throughout the text. Finally, I would like to express my appreciation to two fine editors at McGraw-Hill, John F. Carleo and Kathi A. Benson. Without their enthusiasm and insights this project would still be on the drawing board.

Marvin Karlins

"The No. 1 survival skill for today's business manager is the human relations skill—the ability to understand human behavior and to deal with it intelligently."

Karl Albrecht

The Human Use
of Human Resources

Section One

A Theoretical Orientation

Chapter 1

A Story with a Moral

I will pay more for the ability to deal with people than any other ability under the sun.

John D. Rockefeller

A patient is dying. For 13 years the vital signs have deteriorated—a profile of life ebbing inexorably toward oblivion. Everyone familiar with the case is frustrated; intensive examinations and treatments have done little to alleviate the condition. With time running out, a specialist is called in to save the patient where others have failed. He is advised that the patient is in need of major surgery "to remove the malfunctioning organs and replace them with new ones."

The specialist doesn't agree. He believes that the organs can function effectively without surgery if properly treated. He's right. Three years later the patient's vital signs have clearly improved, and the patient is growing at a healthy, robust rate.

Would it surprise you to find out the patient was a *corporation* and the specialist a *manager?* You most likely know the patient: Avis Rent-A-Car. And the specialist? None other than Robert Townsend, the peppery chief executive who engineered Avis's recovery and wrote about it in his irreverant best-seller *Up the Organization.*[1]

When Townsend took command of Avis in 1962 the floundering company hadn't turned a profit in 13 years of life. The rest is corporate history. In 3 years Avis had more than doubled its sales (from $30 million to $75 million) and amassed earnings in excess of $9 million.

How did Townsend do it? With some unorthodox philosophy, hard work, and a deep, abiding faith in his employees. Claims Townsend:

> When I became head of Avis, I was assured that no one at headquarters was any good, and that my first job was to start recruiting a whole new team. Three years later, Hal Geneen, the President of ITT (which had just acquired Avis), after meeting everybody and listening to them in action for a day, said, "I've never seen such depth of management; why, I've already spotted three chief executive officers!" You guessed it. Same people. I'd brought in only two new people, a lawyer and an accountant.[2]

There was nothing wrong with the "internal organs" of Avis's corporate body—and Townsend knew it. Rather than "cutting out" the people he had, he worked with them, provided them with a corporate environment that satisfied their needs, and encouraged them to be productive. And he succeeded.

There is a profound lesson to be learned from the story of Robert Townsend. It is this: Success or failure in the business world often turns on a manager's ability to utilize human resources effectively (see Box 1-1). Townsend had that ability, and he used it to turn Avis around. When it came to human resource management, Townsend tried harder. He fully understood the need for motivating workers and made the effort to fire them up at work rather than fire them out of work. (Not a bad strategy when you consider that an attempt to dismiss a single federal employee can tie up half of a manager's workday for 18 months at a cost of $100,000 to the taxpayer.[3])

[1]Robert Townsend, *Up the Organization,* Fawcett-Crest, New York, 1970.
[2]Ibid., p. 123.
[3]*Forbes,* July 24, 1978, p. 22 (quoting *Time*).

BOX 1-1

THEY HAD THEIR PIE—AND ATE IT, TOO

History books are bulging with examples of businesses—large and small—which faltered or failed because of poor human resource management. One of the most spectacular examples is also one of the most recent: the bankruptcy of the giant W. T. Grant Company. The executives of this company didn't have a monopoly on poor human resource practices; but if the following quote from *The Wall Street Journal* is true, they went a long way toward establishing a base line against which management incompetence can be measured. Let us hope that their idea of management incentives will be a kind of "custard's last stand."

> Managers for W. T. Grant Co. stores were hit in the face with custard pies or suffered other indignities if they didn't meet their credit quotas.
>
> The hazing procedure was discussed by John E. Sundman, former senior vice president and treasurer of Grant, in his deposition discussing the problems besetting the chain before it went bankrupt.
>
> It was called a Steak and Beans program and had "negative incentives," which consisted of, besides the pie-in-the-face, store managers having their ties cut in half, being forced to run around their stores backward, pushing peanuts with their noses, and not being promoted to larger stores, he said.
>
> Asked if it also had come to his attention that a losing district manager was required to walk around a hotel lobby dressed in nothing but a diaper, Mr. Sundman answered that he had never heard of that one.*

Contrast the human resource practices at the bankrupt Grant's with those of a highly successful company, McDonald's. In another *Wall Street Journal* article, reporter James Hyatt discusses the human use of human resources beneath the "golden arches."

> Individuals deserve a break at McDonald's, the fast-food chain declares.
>
> To preserve the human touch, the corporation creates a "vice president of individuality." The new official, James S. Kuhn,

The Wall Street Journal, Feb. 4, 1977, p. 6.

formerly a personnel officer, says the idea is to "maintain the growth and identity" of the individuals responsible for the company's success. He listens to employee complaints and offers advice. And he tries to consider an employee's personality, as well as abilities, in career planning.

One innovation: an annual "Store Day" when top management from the chairman on down works in restaurants cooking hamburgers and cleaning up, to "keep in touch" with workers. Mr. Kuhn also is studying impact of corporate life on employee families. "We're writing to spouses and some of the older kids for any suggestions," he says.†

†*The Wall Street Journal*, February 1, 1977, p. 1.

JUST HOW IMPORTANT ARE HUMAN RESOURCES IN THE CONTEMPORARY ECONOMY?

Vitally important. Just *how* vital we are only now beginning to appreciate. Unfortunately, early American managers tended to focus most of their energy and attention on developing the production side of management, ignoring or downplaying the human dimension in the workplace. This bias was understandable considering the temper and knowledge of the times. In the first place, "people resources" were plentiful and easily exploitable (rights of labor were yet to be realized). The early managers tended to treat workers much as the early pioneers tended to treat the natural resources on the frontier: as unlimited, cheap, and always replaceable. Conservation of resources just didn't seem relevant in an environment where supply overwhelmed demand and management power over the labor force was so absolute. Secondly, there was the problem of *recognizing* the value of human resources. There was no reason for a manager to grasp the dollar-and-cent value of human resources because profit and loss statements didn't include "people costs" in the balance sheets.[4]

[4]We are just now realizing the significance of this oversight. Recently, for example, twelve executives of a "big board" company tried to assess how much its people really cost. Considering recruiting, hiring and training costs, the amount equaled 75 percent of the corporate net profit before taxes a year earlier. The "people costs" had been hidden because there was no calculation for turnover in the company's financial statements. For an excellent discussion of the financial value of human resources, see J. Rosnow, "Solving the Human Equation in the Productivity Puzzle," *Management Review*, August 1977, pp. 40–43.

In effect, then, the true value of human resources lay hidden—lost in an era of cheap, easily exploitable labor and bookkeeping systems that ignored the impact of human resources in "bottom-line" profit and loss considerations.

How times have changed! Today the effective utilization of human resources is being touted as a major development in maintaining the health of the American economy—a point of view I heartily endorse. Just as our nation has come to understand that the pioneer view of natural resources is no longer viable—that we must now develop a new respect and working plan for our physical environment—so, too, has management come to realize that the early attitudes toward human resources are obsolete and that a new "ecology" of people as a precious commodity must be instituted.

Think of human resource development as a whole new frontier. Unlike production factors, which have been widely explored and developed, human resource development is still largely unexplored and represents a fertile new area for discoveries and progress.

It is imperative that you—a future manager—make the effort necessary to familiarize yourself with this new frontier, so that you may discover how to get the most out of your human resources—how to encourage sustained high levels of productivity at work. This is particularly true today because American business faces foreign challenges unknown in earlier times. If we are to meet successfully the market thrust of other industrialized nations, we must maintain a productive stance at home that will keep us competitive abroad.

Keep in mind the words of management expert Robert Lazer: "If, in fact, the goals of an organization are maintenance and growth, then the productive use of human resources becomes imperative. It is probably in the area of human resource utilization that the greatest short-term improvement in organizational productivity can be obtained."[5]

GETTING THE MOST OUT
OF YOUR HUMAN RESOURCES

Once we recognize the importance of human resources for succeeding in the contemporary business world, the next logical question is, "As a manager, how can I get the most out of the human resources

[5]Robert Lazer, "Behavior Modification as a Managerial Technique," *Conference Board Record,* January 1975, p. 22.

under my direction?'' Or, simply, ''How can I get the most productivity out of my workers?''

The answer to this question will occupy us for the rest of this book. We will be learning to use the motivational techniques developed by behavioral scientists to keep workers productive *and* satisfied. We will also be exploring some new ways of conceptualizing labor-management relations. Before we do this, however, it will be instructive to observe the average working environment, for it is from the contemporary workplace that our strategy of effective human resource management will evolve.

Chapter 2

Work Is a Four-Letter Word

Am I worried about going to hell? Why should I be, I already work there five days a week.

Heavy-equipment operator

Victor Ruiz is a musician residing in Tampa, Florida. He is also a polished amateur golfer with a low handicap and a high degree of dedication to the game. How high? Well, consider one of his rounds as detailed in *Sports Illustrated:*

> Ruiz was going quite well after a few holes at the Rocky Point course. Suddenly pain gripped his chest and he doubled over. His partners suggested that he go back to the clubhouse.
>   "I was playing too good to quit," says Ruiz, "so I hit myself in the gut and the pain went away. I kept on."

The pain came back, but between pars Ruiz slapped at himself some more. He shot 37 on the first nine and was not about to quit. A friend gave him a Coke and some Rolaids.

"I began to feel better," Ruiz recalls, "but soon the pain returned again. This time it was in my arm."

He putted for birdies on the last three holes, making one on the 18th green for 74. Then he all but fell down in a faint. He was rushed home and from there to a hospital, where he was given emergency treatment for the heart attack that had been striking him. He was hospitalized for almost three weeks and is now convalescing.

The incident taught him a lesson, Ruiz says.

"That pain in my arm," he explains, "was one reason I was hitting my long irons so straight. It made me shorten my swing."[1]

Picot Floyd also lives in Tampa, Florida, where he works as a county commissioner. Unfortunately, some of the county employees weren't quite as devoted to their work as Mr. Ruiz was to his golf. Recently, Mr. Floyd attempted to stir his workers from their lethargy with a little "wake-up reminder" called the "Employee Death Tag." The yellow tag suggested:

Because of the close resemblance between death and the normal working attitude in some departments, all supervisors should extend a paycheck as the final test to determine if a worker is really deceased or just snoozing. If the employee does not reach for the paycheck, it reasonably may be assumed that death has occurred.[2]

Things aren't always as they appear, however, and Mr. Floyd cautioned the supervisors: "In some cases, the paycheck-reaching instinct is so strongly developed in the worker that a spasmodic clutching reflex may occur. Don't let this fool you."

Talk about differences in behavior! Mr. Ruiz was highly motivated to pursue his golf game; he played willingly with zest. Contrast this kind of dedication and that of Mr. Floyd's Death Tag recipients, who approached work with all the enthusiasm of bears in hibernation.

Now I am not suggesting that Mr. Floyd's employees throw themselves into their work with reckless abandon—nor, for that

---

[1]Martin Kane, "The Game's the Thing," *Sports Illustrated,* July 24, 1972, pp. 6–7.
[2]Picot Floyd, personal communication, 1978.

matter, do I think Mr. Ruiz should play the links in the midst of a coronary. It would be nice, however, if Commissioner Floyd's yellow-tagged employees could somehow display a bit of Mr. Ruiz's enthusiasm in their work, be a more productive human resource on the job.

Actually, the contrasting behaviors of Mr. Ruiz and the Death Tag employees of Mr. Floyd disturbs those of us involved in the business community. With increasing frequency we observe individuals displaying lackluster performance on the job. What makes matters worse is that many of these listless employees are active, alert, and performing to the best of their ability *outside* the workplace. It is almost as if these individuals possess two personalities: one for weekends and evenings, the other for working hours. Why should this be? Are avocational pursuits inherently more interesting and motivating than work? Is the workplace devoid of challenge and stimulation?

The sad truth is that for an increasing segment of employees work is becoming a four-letter word (see Box 2-1). More and more, labor is seen as an activity to be endured, not enjoyed—an unpleasant necessity of life to be done as quickly as possible and forgotten equally as quickly. Consider, for example, these dismal statistics:

- One poll reports that five out of six workers claim their jobs put them under tension.[3]
- Another survey indicates that about 75 percent of the people who consult psychiatrists are suffering from problems that can be traced to a lack of job satisfaction or an inability to relax.[4]
- Business consultant Ronald Barnes claims that "about half of all working people are unhappy with their careers, and as many as 90 percent may be spending much of their time and energy at jobs that do not help them get any closer to their 'goals in life.' "[5]

A COST WE CAN'T AFFORD

What is the cost of such attitudes and feelings about work? Tremendous, for *both* the nation's economy and its employees. For the individual worker it means the squandering of one-third of a lifetime in

[3] Ronald Kotulak, "Stress: A Small Reward of the Good Life," *Miami Herald,* June 1, 1976, sec. F.
[4] "Cracking Under Stress," *U.S. News & World Report,* May 10, 1976, p. 59.
[5] Ibid.

BOX 2-1

THANK GOD IT'S FRIDAY

Work might be as American as apple pie, but judging from some current employee attitudes, it certainly isn't as enjoyable.

Humorous cartoons are popular vehicles for portraying the very *un*funny condition of contemporary work. For example, judging from the *Frank and Ernest* cartoon included below, do you think the cartoon character will be very enthusiastic about *any* new job?

Consider also the facing "Work Week" sketch. If a picture is worth ten thousand words, this cartoon should tell you a lot about current worker attitudes toward their jobs. In this comic view of labor, the weekend is seen as an oasis, a refuge, a "safe place" where the employee can escape from the miseries of the workplace and store up enough energy to face Blue Monday. Wednesday becomes "hump" day—the day an employee must "get over" to be more than halfway through the workweek. And Friday? It becomes the vestibule to salvation—or as a movie title has suggested: *Thank God It's Friday*.

If you wish to become an *effective* manager, you must learn how to enhance worker satisfaction *and* productivity on the job. This is what skilled human resource management is all about.

FRANK AND ERNEST

Reprinted by permission. © 1978 NEA, Inc.

activity which is distasteful and limiting to personal growth. For American business it means all the evils associated with job dissatisfaction: low morale, absenteeism, reduced productivity, and, in extreme cases, sabotage.

It is a well-established fact that unhappy workers (those whose needs are not being met) are less productive workers; they reduce the ability of American business to survive and prosper in the increasingly competitive world marketplace. In 1972, then Undersecretary of the Treasury Charles E. Walker put it bluntly: "If we don't get increased productivity in this country, we might as well put up a sign saying 'going out of business.' Our economic survival is at stake."[6]

Are things hopeless?

Certainly not! I am firmly convinced that it is possible to create a work environment that will stimulate employees to perform to the best of their ability, to their fullest work potential. And I believe that it is the job and responsibility of management to take the steps necessary to create such a work environment. I call such a workplace a *worthplace,* and it is in this worthplace that we will have the best chance to develop workers who want to work.

[6]Elaine Scott, "Motivation, Productivity and the American Worker," unpublished manuscript, 1978.

Chapter 3

Making the Workplace a Worthplace: The Role of Behavioral Science and the Plus-Plus Relationship

As the next generation of managers it will be your responsibility to create the worthplaces where your employees can reach their full potential as workers and as human beings. To fashion such an environment you must become a *human resource director*, a person who can encourage optimal job performance in your subordinates through *effective leadership* (gaining the respect and cooperation of those you direct) and *motivational practices* (practices that encourage employee productivity and satisfy employee needs).

**THE IMPORTANCE OF BEHAVIORAL SCIENCE
FOR MAKING THE WORKPLACE A WORTHPLACE**

Behavioral science research findings reveal how you can most effectively lead and motivate your employees—how, in short, you can be a successful manager. Combined with on-the-job experience, these

15

findings can help you optimize your human resource skills, assuming, of course, you are willing to use them in the first place (see Box 3-1).

Becoming an effective human resource director is no small accomplishment! As management consultant Karl Albrecht emphasizes: "The #1 survival skill for today's business manager is the human relations skill—the ability to understand human behavior and to deal with it intelligently."[1]

That's *your* survival Albrecht is talking about. And he's right: A

[1]Karl Albrecht, personal communication.

BOX 3-1

SCIENCE FRICTION

Longstanding prejudices and superstitions die hard—like the belief that behavioral science has nothing to contribute to management effectiveness. Some managers really believe this. You can show them actual cases of scientific insights enhancing managerial performance, and they'll nod and smile; then they go right on managing "by the seat of their pants." It's downright maddening. It reminds me of people who would rather wade through a puddle than walk under a ladder and risk "bad luck." You can tell them the ladder idea is superstition, and they'll nod and smile; then, the minute you leave, they'll detour around the ladder as if they hadn't heard a word you said.

A person can afford to walk around ladders, but a manager cannot afford to ignore the scientific insights that lead to superior on-the-job performance. Management theorists Harold Koontz, Cyril O'Donnell, and Heinz Weihrich grasped the importance of behavioral science for effective management in this powerful statement:

Physicians without a knowledge of science become witch doctors; with science, they may be artful surgeons. Executives who attempt to manage without theory, and without knowledge structured by it, must trust to luck, intuition, or what they did in the past; with organized knowledge, they have a far better opportunity to design a workable and sound solution to a managerial problem.*

*Harold Koontz, Cyril O'Donnell, and Heinz Weihrich, *Management*, Seventh Edition, McGraw-Hill, New York, 1980, p. 9.

> For contemporary managers, scientific advances have come none too soon! At the same time workers have gained the power to eliminate some of the older, ethically questionable management practices for controlling job performance, behavioral science has provided new techniques for encouraging high levels of productivity in the workplace.
>
> Gone are the days when managers could simply "pink-slip" unsatisfactory employees, confident that fresh supplies of labor waited to do their bidding. Today's workers are more educated, both in skills and knowledge of their rights. They demand more from their labor than simply a salary, and they know how to get it. They realize that their legal rights make it extremely difficult for management to carry out threats of punishment or dismissal—and that in many cases mediocre work can be sufficient to keep a job. In dealing with these new workers, with their new expectations and powers, behavioral science has given the contemporary manager new ways to stimulate employee productivity and satisfy employee needs on the job.

1979 study by Henchey & Company revealed that 76 percent of the executives in its "outplacement" program lost their jobs because of "difficulties in interpersonal relationships." Only 14 percent of the terminations were attributed to failures in job performance.[2]

PLAYING THE ROLE OF PSYCHOLOGIST

It is recognized in Hollywood that the great movie stars are proficient at playing many different kinds of roles. The same can be said for skilled managers. Throughout your career you will be called upon to play different roles, to wear "different hats" in performing your duties. One of those roles is *psychologist*. As Dr. Harry Levinson has so astutely observed: "We're going to have to go a lot deeper into what makes people tick. Managers will have to know and understand as much about the psychology of motivation as they know about marketing, EDP, and other increasingly functional areas."[3]

[2]Personal communication, 1980.
[3]John Roach, "Managing Psychological Man," *Management Review*, June 1977, p. 27.

Now I am *not* suggesting that to be an effective manager you must be trained as a psychologist to direct the activities of others. Nor, for that matter, am I recommending that you have to be a professional accountant to work with a budget or a trained economist to make company forecasts. What I *am* suggesting is that you gain a basic familiarity with some of the concepts of psychology, accounting, economics, and so forth—so that when the need arises on the job, you will have the information necessary to effectively manage the situation.

Harold Leavitt, managerial psychologist, has argued:

> Some kind of psychological theory is just as necessary for the manager dealing with human problems as is electrical and mechanical theory for the engineer dealing with machine problems. Without theory the engineer has no way of diagnosing what might be wrong when the engine stops, no way of preestimating the effects of a proposed change in design. Without some kind of psychological theory, the manager cannot attach meaning to the red flags of human disturbance; nor can he predict the likely effects of changes in organization or personnel policy.[4]

In Section 2 of this book I will be giving you some of the psychological and behavioral science findings Dr. Leavitt believes you will need to deal most effectively with the human problems you are bound to encounter. We will be focusing on those findings that can be *readily applied* on the job to help you manage your human resources with the highest proficiency—in the words of management pioneer Mary Parker Follett, "get things done through other people." For now it is sufficient for you to recognize the importance of behavioral science findings in helping you develop into a humane and effective manager.

THE SPECTER OF BEHAVIOR CONTROL

A major goal of contemporary psychology is the *control of human behavior*. And, yes, one of *your* major goals as a manager who studies psychological theories and techniques will be to learn how to control

---

[4]Harold Leavitt, *Managerial Psychology*, rev. ed., University of Chicago Press, Chicago, 1964, p. 7.

more effectively the behavior of your subordinates—to get them to do what you want them to do.

Does this sound sinister? Machiavellian? To many of you it might smack of "1984ism" and be repugnant. Yet let me point out that each of you *already* tries to control the behavior of others. The woman who tries to persuade a friend to carry out some task or the man who spanks his child are practicing rudimentary forms of behavior control— rudimentary in comparison with the more sophisticated, effective behavior control techniques used by individuals trained in psychology or in the use of psychologically based behavioral science techniques. You will be learning in this book how to regulate human behavior in a more systematic, scientific, powerful manner—in short, how to control your human resources more effectively.

There is nothing wrong with attempting to control the behavior of others *as long as it is done in a responsible manner.* I do ask you, however, always to remember the following:

I will be giving you information that will make you a more powerful behavior controller (more proficient in your ability to regulate the actions of your employees). With this increased proficiency comes an increasing obligation to use your behavior-changing power in an ethical, humane way—in a manner which will benefit both the behavior controller *and* the controllee. That is what I mean when I speak of the human use (should I say *humane* use?) of human resources.

Sometimes we become so accustomed to our behavior-changing power as to forget we possess it and use it in a careless or callous fashion. This is an unforgiveable error. One can never afford to be casual with behavior-changing power.

Remember that to possess behavior-changing power is both a privilege and a burden. Don't use it unless you are willing to do so in a responsible and ethical way that will benefit your employees as well as you.

ESTABLISHING THE PLUS-PLUS RELATIONSHIP

In the spirit of what I have just said, we come to a major concept in the effective *and* ethical use of behavior control on the job: the creation of the ++ *(plus-plus)* relationship. The ++ (also called *win-win*)

Condition	Management	Labor	Result
"plus-plus" High job productivity High need satisfaction	+	+	"win-win"
"plus-minus" High job productivity Low need satisfaction	+	−	"win-lose"
"minus-plus" Low job productivity High need satisfaction	−	+	"lose-win"
"minus-minus" Low job productivity Low need satisfaction	−	−	"lose-lose"

Figure 3-1 The four possible types of relationships that can occur in the workplace. Management should strive to create the + + (win-win) relationship, as it leads to the greatest worker productivity and satisfaction. The + − (win-lose) and − + (lose-win) relationships can occur for short periods of time, but they create imbalances between the needs of management and labor, usually resulting in the development of a − − condition. This lose-lose relationship occurs, sadly, all too often in the present-day workplace. It should be eliminated if business is to survive.

relationship refers to the establishment of a work environment whereby the needs of management and labor are both fulfilled: specifically, an environment where productivity (management goal) and satisfaction of personal needs (employee goals) coexist (see Figure 3-1).

Why worry about satisfying employee needs anyway? One reason for this emphasis is my belief in human dignity: the assumption that management has a moral obligation to treat people as individuals, not objects. But for those who would label me a "bleeding heart" and rail at the "wastefulness" of this approach, let me emphatically say that such a practice is eminently pragmatic (economically sound).

Study after study, from automobile assembly lines to major department stores, reveals that managers who know how to satisfy workers—how to fulfill their needs—are those who get superior performance from their employees. And no wonder! It has long been known and accepted that to sell your product you must satisfy your customers' needs. Is it so surprising, then, that to sell production to your workers you must satisfy their needs?

The bottom line is clear: humanism and productivity are not incompatible. We can no longer afford to squander our human resources. We must learn to improve the morale and productivity of the workers so that we can effectively compete from a position of strength in the new world economy. Highly respected business expert John Gardner warns that ". . . we must discover how to design organizations and technological systems in such a way that individual talents are used to the maximum, and human satisfaction and dignity are preserved. We must learn to make technology serve man not only in the end product, but in the doing."[5]

Although my appeal for establishing ++ relationships may sound revolutionary, it isn't. As a matter of fact, the ++ concept has been around for quite a while, although judging from current management practices, it seems to have been largely ignored or forgotten. Frederick Taylor, the father of scientific management, had a basic appreciation of the ++ relationship when he spoke of his "mental revolution," in which labor and management would work harmoniously to maximize profits rather than argue about how they should be divided.

The problem is, of course, how you as a manager can go about creating a ++ work environment. It requires a lot of effort, application of the behavioral science principles presented in Section 2, and a belief that work can be something more than a four-letter word. It also involves developing a different conception of the *power relationships* between management and labor, a topic we will turn to in the next chapter. In the meantime you might want to read and ponder the passage in Box 3-2. It seems that young Tom Sawyer had a keen understanding of (and appreciation for) the ++ relationship, which he set out to use in creating a win-win situation on the job.

---

[5]William Dowling, "At General Motors: System 4 Builds Performance and Profits," *Organizational Dynamics,* Winter 1975, p. 37.

BOX 3-2

BRUSHING UP ON THE PLUS-PLUS RELATIONSHIP

Sometimes a job that seems devoid of any satisfaction can, with skillful management, be made to appear in a different light. Case in point: Tom Sawyer and his famous fence-painting encounter. How he got out of doing the job (which he didn't want in the first place) and, most important, got someone else interested in doing it makes interesting reading in the context of the + + relationship.

We pick up the story where Ben, Tom's friend, spots him whitewashing the fence.

"Hello, old chap, you got to work, hey?" Tom wheeled suddenly and said:

"Why, it's you, Ben! I warn't noticing."

"Say—I'm going in a-swimming, I am. Don't you wish you could? But of course you'd druther *work*—wouldn't you? Course you would!"

Tom contemplated the boy a bit, and said: "What do you call work?"

"Why, ain't *that* work?"

Tom resumed his whitewashing, and answered carelessly:

"Well, maybe it is, and maybe it ain't. All I know is, it suits Tom Sawyer."

"Oh, come, now, you don't mean to let on that you *like* it?"

The brush continued to move.

"Like it? Well, I don't see why I oughtn't to like it. Does a boy get a chance to whitewash a fence every day?"

That put the thing in a new light. Ben stopped nibbling his apple. Tom swept his brush daintily back and forth—stepped back to note the effect—added a touch here and there—criticized the effect again—Ben watching every move and getting more and more interested, more and more absorbed. Presently he said:

"Say, Tom, let *me* whitewash a little."

Tom considered, was about to consent; but he altered his mind:

"No—no—I reckon it wouldn't hardly do, Ben. You see, Aunt Polly's awful particular about this fence—right here on the street, you know—but if it was the back fence I wouldn't mind and *she* wouldn't. Yes, she's awful particular about this fence; it's got to be done very careful; I reckon there ain't one boy in a thousand, maybe two thousand, that can do it the way it's got to be done."

"No—is that so? Oh come, now—lemme just try. Only just a little—I'd let *you*, if you was me, Tom."

"Ben, I'd like to, honest injun; but Aunt Polly. . . . If you was to tackle this fence and anything was to happen to it—"

"Oh, shucks, I'll be just as careful. Now lemme try. Say—I'll give you the core of my apple."

"Well, here—No, Ben, now don't. I'm afeard—"

"I'll give you *all* of it!"

Tom gave up the brush with reluctance in his face, but alacrity in his heart. And while . . . Ben . . . worked and sweated in the sun, the retired artist sat on a barrel in the shade close by, dangled his legs, and munched his apple . . .*

*From Mark Twain, *The Adventures of Tom Sawyer,* The Heritage Press, New York, 1936, pp. 26–28.

Chapter 4

A New Conception
of Managerial Power
and Labor-Management
Relations

I believe in power; but I believe that responsibility should go with power.

Theodore Roosevelt

In this chapter I want to talk with you about the power—the ultimate power—to influence human behavior. This brings to mind a demonstration popular in college classrooms. At the beginning of class the professor introduces a Dr. Hans Schmidt to the students, informing them that the guest is a "research chemist of international renown currently employed by the United States government to study the properties of gas diffusion." Dr. Schmidt, clad in a full-length white lab coat and sporting a well-tended goatee, then steps forward and, in a heavy German accent, tells the class he wishes to test the properties of a new chemical vapor he has developed. "Specifically," he says, "I wish to determine how quickly the vapor diffuses throughout the room and how readily people can detect it."

Pointing to a small glass beaker the doctor continues:

> Therefore I would ask your cooperation in a little experiment. I am going to pull this stopper and release the vapor. It is completely harmless but purposely treated to smell like gas—the kind you smell around a stove when the burner doesn't ignite. This particular sample is highly odorous so no one should have any trouble detecting its presence. What I want you to do is raise your hand as soon as you smell the vapor. Are there any questions?

At this point the chemist pulls the stopper and releases the vapor. Very soon, and in a very orderly manner, hands begin going up—first in the front rows and then on back—like a wave rolling through the lecture hall.

Obviously satisfied, the visiting scientist replaces the stopper, thanks the class for its cooperation, and leaves the room. Later on the professor informs his class that the "chemist" was in reality a faculty member from the German Department and the "vapor" nothing more than odorless distilled water.

Why, then, did nearly everyone smell gas? Power of suggestion, you might answer. Certainly the power of suggestion had something to do with it—but that wasn't the only or most important factor at work. Do you think, for example, that a student getting up before the class and making the same appeal could have received the same response as Dr. Schmidt? I've tried it: the answer is no. The power of suggestion worked so well because it was backed up by the *authority* of the person making the suggestion. After all, didn't a famous chemist say the gas would be odorous and readily detected? A *German* chemist at that (we all know how good German scientists are), wearing a white lab coat and referred to by the title of *Dr.* Schmidt.

THE AUTHORITY FIGURE AS A POWER SOURCE

Yes, Dr. Schmidt had all the trappings we associate with an *authority figure*—and a person perceived as an authority can be very persuasive indeed. As a matter of fact, authority figures have tremendous power in our society: they can mold opinions, command obedience, regulate the behavior of others. The most telling and awesome demonstration of this fact was provided by a social psychologist in a series of celebrated experiments at Yale University.

In the early 1960s Dr. Stanley Milgram had been wondering about the role of obedience in man's inhumanity to man, particularly the kinds of inhuman atrocities committed by the Nazis who were "acting under orders." Could the same obedience that made a child dutifully obey his parents and respond in socially acceptable fashion be turned around to make a person commit antisocial acts at the prodding of another authority figure? Dr. Milgram went into his laboratory to find out.

The Milgram experiment was a masterpiece of simplicity and deception. Two subjects were ushered into the laboratory to participate in a "learning experiment, ostensibly designed to study the effect of punishment on memory." One subject was to be the "teacher," the other the "learner." The subjects drew lots to determine their roles, but unbeknown to one of them, the drawing was rigged. One participant, the naive subject, was always given the role of the teacher; the other subject, a confederate of the experimenter, was given the role of the learner.

Once the drawing was completed, the learner was strapped into an "electric chair" and outfitted with electrodes capable of delivering powerful electric shocks to his body. The teacher, after observing this macabre scene, was ushered into an adjacent room containing an intercom and an imposing "shock generator." The generator, an impressive array of dials and switches, was outfitted with a control panel that gave the voltage readings for thirty separate levers (voltage levels went up in 15-volt steps, from 15 to 450 volts). Subjective descriptions of shock intensity were also included on the panel, ranging from Slight Shock at the lower intensities to Danger: Severe Shock at the 400-volt level. To convince the teacher of the authenticity of the shock generator and also to let him experience the painful properties of shock, he was administered a 45-volt stimulation.

The teacher's instructions were quite simple. He was told to teach the learner a list of word pairs over the intercom and punish him with an electric shock whenever he made a mistake, increasing the shock intensity one level (15 volts) for each new mistake. As the experiment progressed, the learner purposely made errors so that the teacher would have to shock him with increasingly severe shocks. As the shock level went up, the learner often made "increasingly insistent demands that the experiment be stopped because of the growing discomfort to him."

Although the teacher didn't realize it, *the learner never received any shocks.* Nor were his pleas real; they were in actuality a tape recording preprogrammed to deliver specific inputs when certain shock levels were reached. "They started with a grunt at 75 volts, proceeded through a 'Hey, that really hurts,' at 125 volts, got desperate with 'I can't stand the pain don't do that' at 180 volts, reached complaints of heart trouble at 195 (the learner had informed the teacher and the experimenter that he had heart trouble before the experiment began), an agonized scream at 285, a refusal to answer at 315, and only heartrending, ominous silence after that."[1]

If the teacher became concerned with the learner's agony, the experimenter ordered him to continue and to disregard the learner's protests. If the teacher balked and tried to quit, the experimenter commanded, "You have no choice, you must go on!" It should be emphasized that the teacher was free to quit the experiment and leave whenever he wanted to; the only way the experimenter could try and keep him at the task was by verbal commands that he must go on.[2]

The teacher's performance score was the highest level of shock intensity he was willing to administer to the learner. Thus his score could range from 0 (unwilling to administer any shock) to 450 (for a subject who gave the highest voltage on the shock generator).

When Dr. Milgram began his experiment, using townspeople from New Haven, Connecticut, he didn't expect many of the teachers to administer very high shocks to the learners. "I'll tell you quite frankly, before I began this experiment, before any shock generator was built, I thought that most people would break off at 'Strong Shock' (135–180 volts) or 'Very Strong Shock' (195–240 volts). You would get only a very, very small proportion of people going out to the end of the shock generator (450 volts), and they would constitute a pathological fringe."[3]

---

[1] P. Meyer, "If Hitler Asked You to Electrocute a Stranger, Would You? Probably," *Esquire,* February 1970, p. 130.

[2] If the teacher expressed concern that he might be held liable for anything that happened to the learner, the experimenter could also attempt to keep him in the study by saying he (the experimenter) would take responsibility for anything that happened.

[3] P. Meyer, op. cit., p. 128

Dr. Milgram's colleagues and his students agreed with his assessment. In fact, when he asked a class of Yale University psychology students to estimate how many of a hypothetical group of a hundred subjects would give the most intense (450-volt) shock, the average answer was 1.2 percent. In other words, the Yale students felt that less than two subjects in a hundred would remain in the experiment to the end.

If only Dr. Milgram and his students had been correct! Unfortunately, their optimistic faith in human nature would find no support in the obedience study. Of the first forty subjects tested not *one* quit the experiment prior to administering 300 volts (at which point the learner is kicking the wall in agony); and twenty-six of the forty teachers (over 60 percent of the subjects tested) obeyed the experimenter to the end, punishing the hapless learner with the full 450 volts.

Many of these teachers displayed extreme tension and misgivings about their behavior, but when prodded on by the stern voice of the experimenter/authority over the intercom, they went on shocking the hell out of the protesting learner.

How much power do authority figures wield in this society? Listen to Dr. Milgram's summary of what he observed in his laboratory: "With numbing regularity, good people were seen to knuckle under to the demands of authority and perform actions that were callous and severe. . . . A substantial proportion of people do what they are told to do, irrespective of the content of the act and without limitations of conscience, so long as they perceive that the command comes from a legitimate authority."[4]

MANAGERIAL AUTHORITY AND POWER

There is no doubt that many people who hold positions of respect and authority can and *do* exert powerful control over the behavior of their fellow citizens. This brings us to the topic of managerial authority and power.

Managers, by the very nature of their position in society, have a degree of authority which gives them power in dealing with their subordinates. There are two reasons for this.

[4]Stanley Milgram, "Some Conditions of Obedience and Disobedience to Authority," *Human Relations*, vol. 18, 1965, pp. 74–75.

    1   The title "manager" carries with it a built-in recognition of legitimate authority, particularly for those working within the business hierarchy.

    2   Managers have a degree of "fate control" over their subordinates (for instance, hiring, firing, promotion, discipline) which lends credence to their position as authority figures.

As a manager you, like Dr. Schmidt and Dr. Milgram, will have the authority to control the behavior of your subordinates to a certain degree, depending in part on how effectively you utilize your power in the work environment.

    But, is a manager's power absolute? That is, can managers control workers' behavior at will—totally, without challenge?

    The answer is no. As a manager you are not the only power factor in a worker's life. There are other persons and institutions that the worker also respects, and those other sources of authority and power can also influence the worker's behavior (see Figure 4-1).

    At various times any or all of these other power sources can influence your employees' behavior; but, for all practical purposes, the only power sources that need concern us here are those of the

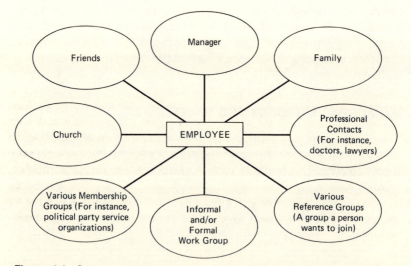

Figure 4-1 Some examples of power sources that can influence a worker's behavior.

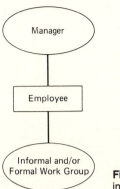

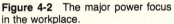

Figure 4-2 The major power focus in the workplace.

manager and the work group (see Figure 4-2). It is between manager and work group that the potential for power conflict and cohesion are greatest; we will therefore examine this most critical relationship in greatest detail.

THE WORK GROUP AS A POWER SOURCE

How many of you have taken a new job and experienced the tug-of-war feeling that occurs when your boss wants you to behave one way and your new coworkers want you to behave another? You're caught right in the middle—a very unpleasant and unfortunately not very uncommon experience.

I vividly remember just such an experience, even though it happened to me long ago. Having taken a summer job on a loading dock, I reported to work the first day and was assigned to load 50-pound sacks of grass seed into a large van. I took to the task with the enthusiasm of a new employee wanting to prove himself to management. Only 2 hours into the workday a fellow employee approached me and suggested that I might be working a bit too fast. This message was delivered in a very effective manner: the 6-foot 6-inch, 250-pound old-timer hoisted all 165 pounds of me into the air and shook me like a rag doll while communicating his recommendation for a work slowdown. Needless to say, I complied with his wishes, and, after checking my body for wear and tear, I returned to the sack loading at a significantly reduced pace. Chalk one up for the work group as a power source!

As a manager you must remember that all groups—including work groups—attempt to regulate members' behavior by the application of rewards and punishments. That is, the individual group member is rewarded for conforming to the standards of the group and punished for deviating from them. Sometimes the rewards and punishments are highly structured, formal, and clearly understood, as in the military. Other times they are more flexible, informal, and open to interpretation, as in the academic profession.

Work groups in industrial plants are notorious for their application of rewards and punishments to keep members in line. These sanctions are so powerful they often take precedence over the reward and punishment system imposed by management in the same plant.

Consider, for example, a classic series of studies at the Hawthorne Division of Western Electric Company in about 1930. One such investigation focused on a bank wiring room, where a group of fourteen workers (nine wiremen, three solderers, and two inspectors) assembled terminal banks for use in telephone exchanges. These workers were paid on the incentive system—the more they produced, the more they were paid.

The assumption behind the wage system was simple enough: every employee would work harder to amass a higher wage. The system failed. Why? Because the informal social organization of the workers in the bank wiring room had established a more powerful set of rewards and punishments (than money) to keep output at a fixed level and successfully challenge the power of management.

In discussing the Western Electric investigations, George C. Homans gives an excellent description of how work-group sanctions operate to control the behavior of individual laborers:

> The working group had also developed methods of enforcing respect for its attitudes. The experts who devised the wage incentive scheme assumed that the group would bring pressure to bear upon the slower workers to make them work faster and so increase the earnings of the group. In point of fact, something like the opposite occurred. The employees brought pressure to bear not upon the slower workers but upon the faster ones, the very ones who contributed most of the earnings of the group. The pressure was brought to bear in various ways. One of them was "binging." If one of the employees did something which was not considered quite proper, one of his fellow workers had the right to

"bing" him. Binging consisted of hitting him a stiff blow on the upper arm. The person who was struck usually took the blow without protest and did not strike back. Obviously the virtue of binging as punishment did not lie in the physical hurt given to the worker but in the mental hurt that came from knowing that the group disapproved of what he had done. Other practices which naturally served the same end were sarcasm and the use of invectives. If a person turned out too much work, he was called names, such as "Speed King" or "The Slave."[5]

WHEN POWERS COLLIDE

On the one hand, you as a manager possess power to influence the actions of your subordinates. On the other hand, work groups also have power which can be brought to bear on employee behavior. You can be sure that at certain times (often many times) during your career, the interests of the work group (or individual workers) and your interests as manager will be "out of sync," in opposition, in conflict. When this happens, we have a situation in which *powers collide*. Such power conflicts will truly test your mettle as a human resource director, for, in the final analysis, skillful handling of your power and the power of your subordinates is what effective managerial leadership is all about. How should you deal with such power problems? What are your options? You have several.

1 You Can Give in to the Opposing Power

What this means, basically, is that you acquiesce to the demands of the work group.[6] At times this is not a bad strategy. Capitulation to work-group power, if done appropriately, can make a manager look flexible, compassionate, and understanding of employees' needs. Also, in the long run of business operations, managers can afford to lose a few skirmishes with employees as long as they win the major battles. I know managers who purposely lose certain labor-management struggles so that they will be in a better position to gain their employees' allegiance on major issues.

[5]G. Homans, "The Western Electric Researches," in Hoslett (ed.), *Human Factors in Management*, Harper, New York, 1951.
[6]In this section I speak of power conflicts between you as manager and the work group; however, these options also hold true in a power conflict between you and an individual worker.

The problem, however, with yielding to work-group demands *too* often is an undermining of managerial power. Managers who consistently adopt the "give in" strategy in labor-management power conflicts are seen as weak and ineffectual, and eventually lose any semblance of authority on the job.

2 You Can Fight Power with Power

Here, the managers' strength is pitted against that of the work group and, as in a tug of war, the strongest power source pulls the opposing force "screaming and dragging their feet" across the finish line. Again, as in the case of the yielding strategy, fighting power with power is a workable policy *at times*. Used properly (and not too often) it can lead to increased worker respect for a manager and also compliance with specified orders.

Now for the difficulties. The problems with pitting power against power are potentially even more lethal than those encountered with the compliance approach. First of all, it can be a tremendous drain of energy for both labor and management, leaving little strength for job-relevant productivity. Secondly, the manager may lose the power struggle, and at that point the manager's authority will be seriously (if not irreparably) damaged. Finally, the manager may win the power battle and still lose the productivity war. Workers who are "beaten" into compliance often exhibit signs of bitterness and hostility long after the power struggle has ostensibly ended. This can lead to all kinds of critical management headaches—including loss of employee morale, reduced productivity, higher absenteeism and job turnover, and in extreme cases even physical confrontations with the manager or sabotage in the workplace.

3 You Can Reach a Compromise with the Opposing Power

Compromise means that nobody is a total winner, but, then, nobody is a total loser either. As a strategy for dealing with power confrontations, compromise can be effective in getting things accomplished and maintaining the peace, particularly if other power alternatives have been attempted and found unsuccessful.

Yet there is a major difficulty with the compromise approach: used too frequently, it often leads to a feeling on the part of management and labor alike that their needs are not being met. One business manager put it this way: "Compromise is a lot like having Chinese food—you eat it, but ten minutes later you feel hungry again."

4   You Can Harness the Opposing Power

When you harness the opposing power, you are basically using it to accomplish your own goals. This is not easily achieved, but if it can be done, it is the *best* way to deal consistently with conflicts of power.

In a business context the best method of harnessing the opposing power is to convince workers or work groups that it is in their best interest to carry out the actions that you, the manager, wish them to perform. Tom Sawyer did this with a flourish in the example presented in Box 3-2 (see pp. 21–23). You will be able to do it, too, once you put into practice the behavioral science techniques you will be learning in Section 2.

Harnessing employee power for your own ends might seem strange and new in business, but there is, in fact, nothing unusual or novel in this approach. There are many physical and human examples of this process—for instance, in the harnessing (with dams) of water power for electricity or the use of solar energy to heat homes and offices. Practitioners of the martial arts have long recognized that you can turn another person's power to your service. Thus, an individual skilled in the art of self-defense will readily utilize the attacking thrust of an adversary's arm to help throw the opponent off balance or to the ground.

HARNESSING POWER AND THE PLUS-PLUS RELATIONSHIP

In Chapter 3 I spoke of the need to establish a ++ relationship in the workplace—a condition whereby the needs of management and labor are both fulfilled; specifically, a condition in which productivity (management goal) and need satisfaction (employee goal) coexist. I suggested that until the ++ goal was met, relations between labor and management would be strained and work would continue to be viewed as a four-letter word.

In the present discussion, you can now see how important establishment of the ++ relationship becomes. Without the development of this win-win environment, suspicion and hostility between employee and employer will persist. As a matter of fact, the idea of harnessing worker power seems so farfetched in the business world exactly because of the antagonistic historical relationship that has evolved between manager and subordinate—making the idea of mutual cooperation seem unworkable, even unthinkable.

As long as this "adversarial" posture endures, the chance of harnessing worker power will remain remote. There will be too much distrust, too much hostility, too much of a win-lose attitude. It is only through the creation of the ++ relationship that the old conceptions will give way to a more cooperative labor-management relationship, paving the way for you as future managers to harness worker power in the service of higher productivity.

A NEW MODEL FOR LABOR-MANAGEMENT RELATIONS

Steps must be taken, and taken now, to find the formula for establishing the ++ relationship, for reducing conflict between labor and management—a productivity-draining interaction we can no longer afford in the light of current economic realities. One person who has taken such a step—and it is a giant one—is Muzafer Sherif, who, like Stanley Milgram, is a social psychologist. In the 1950s, Dr. Sherif conducted an innovative experiment with groups that, in my opinion, represents the most important psychological contribution ever made to the understanding of how to reduce hostility between labor and management and establish a healthy ++ business environment. First let me present the experiment, and then I'll discuss its importance for contemporary management-labor relations.

The Sherif Experiment

Every year hundreds of thousands of city kids make their annual migration to that treasured American institution, the summer camp. There they swim, fish, shoot, canoe, learn arts and crafts, and go on overnights. At a camp in Oklahoma they unknowingly became experimental subjects in Dr. Sherif's study of intergroup relations.

A psychology experiment in a summer camp? It sounds strange. Yet, in actuality, Dr. Sherif chose this particular "laboratory" for sound scientific reasons: isolated from the outside world, the summer campsite provided a place where scientific control could be more readily achieved, a place where Sherif and his staff could manipulate the environment and observe the campers in a naturalistic setting, without fear that disturbances from the outside world would confound their results.

The campers that Sherif chose for his experiment were a counselor's dream: twenty-two healthy, well-adjusted 11-year-old boys, all from stable, middle-class families and in the upper half of their classes in scholastic standing. None of the boys had been problem children at home, in the neighborhood, or in school. They were basically peaceful preteenagers. Yet in a matter of weeks, they would be aggressively embroiled in a full-scale camp war under the watchful eye of the camp staff.

The camp war did not occur accidentally. It was an outgrowth of carefully planned experimental manipulations designed to help Dr. Sherif answer two basic questions: (1) How does intergroup conflict arise? (2) How can such conflict be reduced? In answering these inquiries, Dr. Sherif divided his camp study into three basic parts.

1   Stage of Group Formation   Before you can study intergroup relations, you have to have groups. In the group-formation stage, two independent cohesive groups were created. This involved, first, an attempt by Dr. Sherif and his staff to divide the twenty-two campers into two equal units, making sure that the physical skills and sizes of the campers were roughly equivalent in each unit. Once this was done, the boys were transported, in separate buses, to opposite ends of the campsite and billeted in separate cabins. Then, for about a week the boys in each cabin participated in activities designed to foster the growth of well-developed groups. These activities included canoe trips over rough terrain and cookout overnights, the kinds of highly appealing tasks that require concerted, cooperative effort to carry out and build esprit de corps among the participants. Once each cabin unit had developed into a well-defined group, both groups were brought together for the first time, and the second stage of the experiment commenced.

2   Stage of Intergroup Conflict   Just as you cannot study intergroup relations without groups, neither can you study the reduction of intergroup conflict without first producing that conflict. The question is, "How do you go about producing conflict between

two groups of campers who are basically well-behaved and peaceful?" Dr. Sherif gives us an important hint with the following
hypothesis:

> When members of two groups come into contact with one another in a
> series of activities that embody goals which each urgently desires, but
> which can be attained by one group only at the expense of the other,
> competitive activity toward the goal changes, over time, into hostility
> between the groups and their members.[7]

Now what "series of activities" can be conducted at a summer
camp that "embody goals which each [group] urgently desires, but
which can be attained by one group only at the expense of the other"?
For those of you who have been to camp, one answer probably comes
to mind immediately: a color war. For those unfamiliar with this term,
a color war is a kind of junior Olympics, a time when the camp is
divided into teams (each team designated by a color) that compete in a
series of athletic events lasting from a day to a week or more. When all
the events are completed, the team with the highest total score wins
the color war. As any camper or counselor who has gone through such
an experience will attest, a color war creates a fierce sense of
competition and team pride that permeates the whole camp while the
contest is in progress.

Making use of the color war potential for creating intergroup
hostility, Dr. Sherif and the camp staff arranged for the boys of the two
cabins to oppose each other in a tournament that included baseball,
football, tent pitching, and tug-of-war contests. Observes Dr. Sherif:

> The tournament started with a great deal of zest and in the spirit of good
> sportsmanship to which these American boys had already been thor-
> oughly indoctrinated. . . . As the tournament progressed from event to
> event, the good sportsmanship and good feeling began to evaporate. The
> sportsman-like cheer for the other group, customarily given after a game,
> "2-4-6-8, who do we appreciate," turned to a derisive chant: "2-4-6-8,
> who do we appreci*hate*."[8]

[7]M. Sherif and C. Sherif, *Social Psychology*, Harper & Row, New York, 1969, p.
239.
[8]Ibid., p. 240.

In a very short time, what had begun as friendly relations between two groups of peaceful boys deteriorated into an intercabin donnybrook, replete with name-calling, fisticuffs, cabin raids, and property destruction. Dr. Sherif notes: "If an outside observer had entered the situation after the conflict began . . . he could only have concluded on the basis of their behavior that these boys (who were the 'cream of the crop' in their communities) were either disturbed, vicious, or wicked youngsters."[9] That's how bad things got.

There was no question about it: Intergroup conflict had been solidly achieved at Dr. Sherif's summer camp. The problem now was to end it. The whole purpose of the experiment was to find a way of reducing intergroup conflict; and judging from the behavior of Dr. Sherif's campers, there would never be a better time to find the solution.

3 Reduction of Intergroup Conflict Through experimental manipulation, Dr. Sherif had first created conditions conducive to the formation of groups and then to the onset of hostilities between them. Now, in the final stage of the experiment, Dr. Sherif set out to answer this question: "How can two groups in conflict, each with hostile attitudes and negative images of the other and each desiring to keep the members of the detested outgroup at a safe distance, be brought into cooperative interaction and friendly intercourse?"

Several approaches were tried. One approach was an *appeal to the moral values* shared by members of both groups. This appeal was contained in sermons given by the camp minister at religious services. In these sermons, he talked of brotherly love, the value of cooperation, and the need for forgiving one's enemies. "The boys arranged the services and were enthusiastic about the sermons," Dr. Sherif writes. Nevertheless, "upon solemnly departing from the ceremony, they returned within minutes to their concerns to defeat, avoid, or retaliate against the detested outgroup."[10]

A second approach involved *bringing the groups together at events that were very enjoyable.* Thus, the groups were brought

[9]Ibid., p. 254.
[10]Ibid., p. 254.

together to eat, see movies, shoot off fireworks on the Fourth of July, and so forth. Unfortunately, this approach also failed. "Far from reducing conflict, these situations served as occasions for the rival groups to berate and attack each other. . . . The mealtime encounters were dubbed 'garbage wars' by the participants,"[11] who used their food for ammunition rather than nourishment.

The one approach that Dr. Sherif believed would work—*and did*—involved the use of *superordinate goals* in the reduction of intergroup conflict. "Superordinate goals are those goals that have a compelling appeal for members of each group, but that neither group can achieve without participation of the other."[12]

To demonstrate that accomplishing superordinate goals leads to reduced intergroup hostility, Dr. Sherif and his staff rigged the camp program so that highly desirable activities and outcomes could be realized only through the joint cooperation of the two groups. For example, one day on an outing, the two groups of boys were faced with a terrible problem: Hot, tired, and hungry, they reached their campsite only to discover that the truck which was to go for food and water was stalled and needed to be pulled onto the road. One group of campers got a rope, tied it around the truck's fender, and began to tug. The vehicle didn't move, and it became obvious that one group working alone couldn't accomplish the task. When both groups pulled on the rope together, however, they were able to get the truck started and on its way.

Joint efforts in situations such as the stalled truck episode did not immediately dispel hostility between the two groups. "But gradually," Dr. Sherif notes, "the series of activities requiring interdependent action reduced conflict and hostility between the groups. . . . In the end, the groups were actively seeking opportunities to intermingle, to entertain and 'treat' each other."[13]

All's well that ends well. On the last day of the camp session, the boys were given the choice of returning home together on one bus or on two separate buses, one for each group. They voted to return together.

[11]Ibid., p. 256.
[12]Ibid.
[13]Ibid.

SUPERORDINATE GOALS AND
LABOR-MANAGEMENT RELATIONS

From peace to war and back to peace again. At least in his summer camp, Dr. Sherif seemed to create conflict or cooperation at his bidding. Now nobody is suggesting that what Dr. Sherif did with a group of boys in Oklahoma he could do as easily with labor and management. But what Dr. Sherif learned about the induction and reduction of intergroup hostility might very well be applicable to improving labor-management relations.

In contemporary business, we are confronting productivity problems that can be solved only through the *cooperation* of labor and management. Just as Dr. Sherif's campers could not move the truck without intergroup cooperation, neither can we move the economy forward without the cooperation of employer and employee working together.

This currently leaves us in an extremely ironical state of affairs. Labor and management are, in fact, partners in progress—they are irrevocably yoked together in a common effort to survive and prosper. One can not succeed without the other. Yet, through the years these two groups have behaved as if they were natural foes, enemies to be defeated.

Please don't get me wrong. I am not saying that it is unhealthy or unnatural to allow an "adversarial" position between labor and management (the Western nations have squabbles even though they are allies). Disagreements and differences of opinion can be healthy to all parties, if carried out in the proper spirit and context. What I am saying is that as future managers your perception of labor-management relations (one you should attempt to transmit to labor and one which labor should embrace as well) should be more in keeping with the true reality of the situation. Labor and management are like Siamese twins, joined together in a struggle for survival. You can't cut off one half and expect the other half to survive and prosper.

Management and labor should think in terms of cooperation rather than conflict, harmony rather than tension. Business presents employer and employee with a "natural" superordinate goal. It would be a shame if labor and management didn't grasp at the opportunity to cooperate in the achievement of that goal.

Remember the all-important Sherif hypothesis:

When members of two groups come into contact with one another in a series of activities that embody goals which each urgently desires, but which can be attained by one group only at the expense of the other, competitive activity toward the goal changes, over time, into hostility between the groups and their members.[14]

It would be the height of unnecessary tragedy if labor and management waste their energy fighting each other on the mistaken assumption that only one group can win at the expense of the other, when in fact the only way either group can win is through the mutual cooperation of both.

As long as management and labor insist on viewing their interaction in terms of a win-lose situation, only a lose-lose result can occur, particularly in today's world, where business faces harsher international competition than ever before. When, on the other hand, both groups come to see their roles as cooperative, interdependent, and win-win in nature, then the potential for a productive ++ relationship will be enhanced, along with the opportunity for management to effectively harness worker power in the service of higher productivity (see Box 4-1).

[14]Ibid., p. 239.

BOX 4-1

**AN EXAMPLE OF COOPERATION
IN LABOR-MANAGEMENT RELATIONS**

Sometimes it takes a crisis to move labor and management from an "adversarial" position to one of cooperation. As discussed in the following excerpt from an article in *Time* magazine, just such a crisis occurred at the General Motors Corporation's factory in Tarrytown, New York, and just such a cooperative effort was undertaken. The results of the effort speak well for a superordinate approach to labor-management relations.

STUNNING TURNAROUND AT TARRYTOWN*

American-made automobiles last week were again selling like Edsels. Mid-April car sales by General Motors, Ford and Chrysler dropped 32% from the same period a year earlier. Detroit continues to struggle with the dark reputation that it turns out cars inferior to those made by Japanese or West German manufacturers and that American workers are not sufficiently productive. But one Big Three plant belies such notoriety. The General Motors factory in Tarrytown, N.Y., one of the plants where the company assembles its hot-selling front-wheel-drive Chevrolet Citations, has earned the reputation of being perhaps the giant automaker's most efficient assembly facility. Tarrytown's current renown is more surprising because in the early 1970s the 55-year-old plant was infamous for having one of the worst labor-relations and poorest quality records at GM.

The turnaround at Tarrytown grew out of the realization by local management and union representatives that inefficiences and industrial strife threatened the plant's continued operation. Automakers sometimes use forced plant closings caused by sluggish auto sales to unload a lemon facility. Ford, for example, decided two weeks ago to shut the gates of its huge Mahwah, N.J., plant largely because it had a poor quality record. After Tarrytown lost a truck production facility in 1971, bosses and workers became fearful for their jobs and got together to find better ways to build cars. At first hesitantly but later with enthusiasm, they embarked on an unusual joint experiment to improve work and to tap shop-floor expertise for running the factory.

The setting for the initiative could hardly have been more dismal. Some 7% of the plant's workers were regularly failing to appear for work, and the number of outstanding employee grievances against management totaled 2,000. The result of the confrontation and conflict was sloppy work, rapidly rising dealer complaints, and an unprecedented number of disciplinary and dismissal notices. "Workers and bosses were constantly at each other's throats," recalls Gus Beirne, then general superintendent of the plant. Agrees Larry Sheridan, the former United Auto Workers shop chairman at Tarrytown: "It sure as hell was a battleground."

The first significant payoff from the new mood at the plant came at model changeover time in 1972 and then again the following year. GM management showed workers the proposed changes in the assembly line and invited their comments. Says Beirne: "A lot of good ideas came forward, and we were shown a lot of problems we didn't realize existed. Things we had missed were picked up, and we had time to implement them before the start of the new models."

The cost savings produced by simply sharing information with the shop floor encouraged Tarrytown's executives to move further. In 1972, the plant's supervisors began holding regular meetings with workers on company time to discuss worker complaints and ideas for boosting efficiency. In order to turn the gripe sessions into something more substantive, both sides agreed to bring in an outside consultant to organize worker-participation projects. They chose Sydney Rubinstein, 52, a former blue-collar tool-and-die worker and white-collar engineer, who had become an expert on worker innovation and productivity.

Rubinstein's first breakthrough came in a trial project with Tarrytown's 30 windshield installers. Half of the workers had been disciplined during the previous six months for poor work. During discussions it was revealed that each worker selected a different point around the windshield to begin applying the sealant. One worker explained that he started at the spot where the radio antenna wires emerged from the windshield because "you get a little extra adhesive, a puddle, and that stops leaks." That little trick was new to the other workers, the foreman and the plant engineers. The method was immediately adopted and resulted in a rapid reduction in the number of dealers' complaints. Later, the plant's body-shop workers held informal discussions on welding problems. Within a few months, the percentage of bad welds dropped from 35% to 1.5%. When the small voluntary program of worker participation was expanded to the plant's 3,800 employees, 95% of them took part. The plan eventually cost GM $1.5 million.

As a result of these projects, workers say, they now readily inform supervisors that they would rather discuss problems than knock heads. "The evolution that has taken place is terrific," says Ray Calore, president of the local U.A.W. "There are no longer any hidden-ball tricks. If management has a problem, we sit and discuss it." The U.A.W. insists that job-participation programs like those at Tarrytown are neither a panacea to end all labor disputes nor just a management tool to boost output. But giving workers a greater voice in their job can improve productivity by bringing about declines in grievances, absenteeism and waste.

The benefits of the new attitudes are clear. Since 1976, the Tarrytown plant has turned out high-quality products. There are now only about 30 outstanding worker grievances, while absenteeism has fallen by two-thirds, to 2.5%. Disciplinary orders, firings, worker turnover and breakage all show significant declines. The clear lesson from Tarrytown is that both management and workers can cooperate to their mutual advantage to boost job satisfaction and increase productivity. Says Dartmouth Business Administration Professor Robert H. Guest: "Tarrytown represents in microcosm the beginnings of what may become commonplace in the future—a new collaborative approach on the part of management, unions and workers to improve the quality of life at work in its broadest sense."

GETTING THINGS STARTED

The road leading to harmonious, productive relations between labor and management will be long and, at times, treacherous. In a sense, I envision each of you as an "Ambassador of Goodwill," sent out on a mission to reduce the distrust and hostility built up between labor and management in the past. Being apprised of the necessity for creating a + + relationship in the workplace is the first step in your journey. The second step involves acceptance of the superordinate approach to business success. The third step involves the application of behavioral science findings to enhance worker productivity and satisfy worker needs. Learning how to take that third step will occupy our attention as we turn now from theory to practice: the actual things you can do to be a more effective manager on the job.

How to Be an Effective Human Resource Manager in the Real World

Chapter 5

The Need to Know

The need to know is your employee's need.

First-line supervisor

Having just finished the theoretical section of this book, you now have a philosophical and conceptual basis for effective human resource management. But, I hear you asking, how can I apply that theory in practice and make myself a more effective manager on the job? In other words, how do I translate theoretical ideas into action programs in the workplace?

The answer is, by utilizing behavioral science techniques to satisfy worker needs and enhance worker output. I will be discussing these techniques in the next few chapters, showing you how to use them to harness worker power and create the ++ relationship so vital to making the workplace a productive worthplace. First, however, you must know the following.

HOW TO UNDERSTAND AND IDENTIFY
INDIVIDUAL WORKER NEEDS

Before you can satisfy worker needs, you must know what they are. If you think you already do, then spend a moment to take the test in Box 5-1.

BOX 5-1

TEST DIRECTIONS

Below, you will find a list of 10 things people want from their work. Your task is to rank the items in order from 1 (most important) to 10 (least important) on the basis of how you think the average worker (*not* manager) would rate the items. In other words, try to predict how a worker would respond to the 10 items on the basis of their job-related needs.

Here are the 10 items. Remember, 1 is most important, 10 is least important.

YOUR ESTIMATE OF WORKER'S RANKING	WHAT PEOPLE WANT FROM THEIR WORK
_____	Full appreciation of work done
_____	Feeling of being in on things
_____	Sympathetic help on personal problems
_____	Job security
_____	Good wages
_____	Interesting work
_____	Promotion and growth in the organization
_____	Personal loyalty to employees
_____	Good working conditions
_____	Tactful disciplining

Once you have finished taking the test (and not before!) I think you'll find it instructive to look at two other sets of responses shown here: one from an actual group of employees, the other from a group of supervisors. Put your own estimates in the blanks provided and then make a few comparisons.

The employee rankings represent the actual expression of what a group of workers felt were important wants to be satisfied on the job. How did you do in comparison with their rankings? Did you

What people want from their work	Employee ranking	Supervisor ranking	Your ranking
Full appreciation of work done	1	8	_____
Feeling of being in on things	2	10	_____
Sympathetic help on personal problems	3	9	_____
Job security	4	2	_____
Good wages	5	1	_____
Interesting work	6	5	_____
Promotion and growth in the organization	7	3	_____
Personal loyalty to employees	8	6	_____
Good working conditions	9	4	_____
Tactful disciplining	10	7	_____

accurately assess what they wanted most from their work? If you didn't, don't feel bad—you weren't alone. When you glance at the supervisors' ranking it's obvious that they, too, were way off when it came to guessing what workers want most on the job.

Commenting on these data, Professor Kenneth Kovach notes:

> The ranking of items is not necessarily the important thing to observe, since conditions have changed since . . . the survey was taken. The significant point is the wide variance between what workers consider to be important in their jobs and what their supervisors think workers believe to be important. Research indicates that a wide gap still exists between what workers want from their jobs and what management thinks they want.[1]

Unfortunately, it has been this management misreading of worker needs that has led to so many problems in labor-management relations now and in the past.

As I indicated earlier, to increase worker productivity you must satisfy worker needs, and to satisfy worker needs you must know what

[1]Kenneth Kovach, "Improving Employee Motivation in Today's Business Environment," *MSU Business Topics*, Autumn 1976, p. 7.

they are. Different workers have different needs at different times. If you can ascertain each employee's needs with accuracy, you'll be in a better position to satisfy the employee and encourage higher productivity on the job.

Assessing the needs of individual workers is not as difficult as it sounds. In the first place, many workers have the same needs. Then, there aren't that many different needs to worry about. Moreover, by conscientiously observing your employees you can usually ascertain their needs. Finally, behavioral scientists have provided us with some good "models" of human needs, models that will help you understand and assess workers' needs more accurately. Here I would like to present one such model: the so-called need hierarchy of Abraham Maslow.[2] Although the model is a gross oversimplification of complex human behavior and doesn't hold true for every employee you'll confront, it still provides us with some useful guidelines for identifying worker needs and understanding how they operate.

THE MASLOW MODEL OF HUMAN NEEDS

Think for a moment: If I were to ask you to explain your behavior—to tell me why you pursued a certain goal or acted in a certain way—how would you answer? Abraham Maslow spent a career considering this kind of question, and here is how he would reply:

1 People have needs and they will act in ways to satisfy their needs. As long as our needs remain unfulfilled they act as *motivators,* stimulating us to behave in ways that will lead to the satisfaction of those needs. Once a need is satisfied, however, it no longer motivates a person and other unfulfilled needs take its place.

2 Some needs are more pressing (more important) than others. For instance, the need to breathe is more crucial than the need to gain public recognition for a job well done.

3 The basic, most survival-relevant needs must first be satisfied before other, more psychologically oriented needs become motivators of behavior. In other words, a person will seek to satisfy the rumblings of an empty stomach before turning to the challenges of an inquisitive mind.

[2]Abraham Maslow, *Motivation and Personality,* Harper, New York, 1954.

It was Maslow's realization that human needs vary in importance and behavioral priorities which led him to postulate his "need hierarchy" concept (see Figure 5-1).

It will help you understand the need hierarchy if you view it as a kind of stepladder people climb on their way to total fulfillment as human beings.

The first rung on the ladder represents the *physiological needs*. These are very urgent needs that must be satisfied before any higher-rung needs can come into play. There are very few physiological needs, but they must be satisfied if the individual is to survive. Examples of these needs are air, water, food, and—in certain climates—clothing and shelter. In contemporary North America most people have been successful in satisfying their survival needs; but for the millions of people throughout the world who haven't, life is little more than a grim day-by-day struggle for survival.

The second rung on the ladder represents the *safety needs*. Once

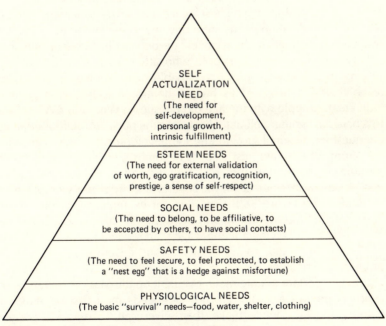

SELF
ACTUALIZATION
NEED
(The need for
self-development,
personal growth,
intrinsic fulfillment)

ESTEEM NEEDS
(The need for external validation
of worth, ego gratification, recognition,
prestige, a sense of self-respect)

SOCIAL NEEDS
(The need to belong, to be affiliative, to
be accepted by others, to have social contacts)

SAFETY NEEDS
(The need to feel secure, to feel protected, to establish
a "nest egg" that is a hedge against misfortune)

PHYSIOLOGICAL NEEDS
(The basic "survival" needs—food, water, shelter, clothing)

Figure 5-1 Maslow's hierarchy of human needs.

people have won the day-to-day struggle to stay alive, they start looking for longer-term solutions to the survival problem. People with safety needs are motivated to seek *security:* to protect themselves against misfortune and put distance between themselves and the daily scramble for survival.

The third rung on the ladder represents the *social needs.* Here the individual is concerned with *affiliation:* being around other people and being accepted by them. People with social needs want to belong—they desire social relationships and the chance to interact with others.

The fourth rung on the ladder represents *esteem needs.* People with esteem needs seek external validation of their worth; that is, they want others to recognize their competence and accomplishments. Individuals with these "ego" needs are concerned with prestige, status, and a sense of self-respect that comes with recognized achievement.

The fifth rung on the ladder is *self-actualization* and represents, according to Maslow, the highest level of human development. People with self-actualization needs are motivated to seek internal validation of their worth; that is, their values are defined in terms of personal beliefs and philosophies. People who attempt to self-actualize are striving to become all they are capable of becoming—in short, to reach their full potential as human beings. It is in this stage that individuals grapple with the age-old questions: Who am I? Where am I? Where am I going? Self-actualization is the pursuit of self-fulfillment, the quest for personal growth and the development of the total self.

From what I have just said, it becomes evident that a person's position on the Maslow hierarchy will determine, in large part, what that person wants out of life in general and from the workplace in particular (see Figure 5-2). Consider, for example, a person on the "first rung" of the Maslow hierarchy. Certainly this individual will be more satisfied receiving a living wage than recognition as "employee of the month." And, as we know, a satisfied employee is a more productive employee.

It is important to note that movement up the Maslow hierarchy of needs is progressive; that is, "lower" needs must first be satisfied before "higher" needs make themselves felt. Further, if people operating at a higher need level are suddenly confronted by conditions which push them back to a lower level, then those lower needs will

What a Person Wants out of Life	Maslow's Hierarchy of Needs	What a Person Wants out of a Job
Freedom Personal growth (self-development) Achieve full human potential	Self-actualization needs	Creative and challenging work Responsibility for decision making Flexibility and freedom
Status Prestige Recognition for achievement	Esteem needs	Promotion Praise (recognition) by supervisor Merit pay increase
Social relationships Acceptance by others Affiliation	Social needs	Compatible work group Social activities at work Friendship at work
Security Safety "Nest egg"	Safety needs	Safe and healthy working conditions Job security Reasonable wages and fringe benefits
Food Water Clothing and shelter	Physiological needs	Meals Shelter from the elements Subsistence wages

Figure 5-2 What people want out of life and work at various levels of Maslow's need hierarchy.

once again predominate. An example: Suppose you're a wealthy businessperson who functions at the esteem level of human needs. One afternoon your pleasure boat is blown out to sea and suddenly you're forced to fight for survival on a day-to-day basis. Under such conditions you would revert to functioning at the level of physiological needs until the crisis was resolved.[3]

Some Limitations of the Maslow Model

As I pointed out earlier, Maslow's need hierarchy isn't a precise scientific instrument for predicting human behavior; rather, it is a descriptive model that gives us general guidelines for classifying and understanding human needs.

When considering Maslow, you should be aware that not all people behave according to his model. For instance, some people are motivated by more than one need at a time—like the person who strives for social relationships (social need) and prestige (esteem need) at the same time. There are also people who don't fit into the five-step progression of needs in the need hierarchy. Some people skip over certain need levels entirely (as when a person moves from safety

[3]For a good example of what happens when people are suddenly thrust into a survival situation read Paul Piers, *Alive*, Lippincott, Philadelphia, 1974.

needs directly to esteem needs); others voluntarily move *down* the need hierarchy (for instance, well-paid executives who quit their jobs in favor of subsistence farming on an agricultural commune). Finally, there is the factor of *rising expectations*.

> As people partially satisfy each need, they tend to require more of it for full satisfaction. This . . . phenomenon of rising expectations . . . partially explains why workers today are unhappy with their earnings even though earnings have never been higher. A starving factory worker of the 1800s was overjoyed to earn enough to buy an extra potato. A factory worker today becomes angry if he cannot afford steak.[4]

So much for the limitations of the Maslow model. Even with such shortcomings, it can still be an extremely valuable ally in your efforts to manage more effectively. Do, however, keep those limitations in mind.

Using Maslow to Manage

A basic premise of this book can be expressed in the statement: *if you want worker productivity you must satisfy worker needs.* I began this chapter by suggesting that many contemporary managers can't satisfy worker needs because they don't know what they are. I then presented the Maslow model to help you understand the types of human needs and how they function, an understanding that should put you in a better position to identify your workers' needs more accurately. Let me explain why this is so.

Based on what Maslow has said, you now know the types of needs workers have and the corresponding factors that can be used to satisfy those needs on the job (Figure 5-2). Further, you realize that once a need is satisfied it ceases to motivate a person and other needs "take over." Finally, you are now aware that a person normally satisfies needs step by step, starting with the basic physiological (survival) needs and moving up to the psychological needs of esteem and self-actualization.

Given this information, plus your knowledge of current economic conditions, you might well decide that most contemporary American workers will be motivated by higher (as opposed to lower) level needs. And you would be right (see Box 5-2). Of course, this wasn't always

[4]Michael Mescon and David Rachman, *Business Today,* Random House, New York, 1976, p. 159.

BOX 5-2

HOW BOSSES GET PEOPLE TO WORK HARDER*

Despite inflation's bite, most workers put job satisfaction ahead of a raise, says a noted industrial psychologist, Arthur Witkin. He asserts that recognition by the boss, the opportunity to participate in management decisions and a feeling that one's work is useful are more important in motivating employees than is salary or job security. Management often doesn't get its money's worth from fringe benefits, he adds, and promotions aren't always welcomed.

The following is an excerpt, reprinted from *U.S. News and World Report,* from an interview with Witkin, who is chief psychologist for the Personnel Sciences Center in New York City and an associate professor at Queens College.

Q: Professor Witkin, how do people's attitudes toward their jobs differ from attitudes in the past?

A: Workers today are far more interested in personal satisfaction, in "doing their own thing." They put less stress on cash pay and on long-term job security. They are motivated by far more complex things than was true of jobholders a generation or so ago.

The greatest mistake management can make is to fail to understand this complexity of motivation. Often an employer will say: "Workers want money. We'll pay them more, and that will do the trick." Of course, that doesn't do the trick. It's the sort of thing that might work with Pavlov's dogs—where you have a simple stimulus-response relationship—but it won't work with humans.

Q: What accounts for the marked change in work attitudes recently?

A: A whole series of factors have come into play: Our country has a higher level of education than ever before, and a higher standard of living. Youngsters are more sophisticated; they want to throw off parental shackles and get away from school discipline. And, of course, none of today's young people has had any contact with an economic setback as severe as the Depression of the 1930s.

*Excerpt from an interview with Arthur Witkin, "How Bosses Get People to Work Harder," *U.S. News & World Report,* Jan. 29, 1979, pp. 63–64. Copyright 1979 U.S. News & World Report, Inc.

The result of all this is that younger workers feel they can pretty much call their own tune on a job; if they don't like what they see, they'll pick up their marbles and walk away. They figure they can always find something else, or maybe collect unemployment insurance.

Q: Has the rise of two-income families spurred the idea of worker independence?

A: I'm sure it has. If one partner wants to change jobs, it's not the traumatic situation that it would be if there were only a single breadwinner.

It's no longer as hard to survive in this country as it was years ago. Workers once were so preoccupied with making enough money to provide food and to keep a roof over their heads that they never had time to contemplate whether there was anything beyond that—something more to the job than just earning a living. Today's affluence has made all the difference. And, of course, the job-satisfaction idea cuts two ways: A working wife wants to be happy at work just as does her husband.

Q: How can management deal with this?

A: Perhaps the single most important thing is to be aware of a worker's need for self-esteem. Everyone needs to feel good about himself; if he doesn't, he'll not only turn in a poor job performance, he'll keep others from doing their best.

One way to deal with this involves worker participation in decisions that concern them. Some matters, for instance, must be solely a management prerogative, such as where a new plant should be located; but there are many other decisions in which workers can be given a say.

the case. In earlier times, when labor rights were nonexistent and wages desperately low, workers could not have cared less about prestige or the opportunity for self-esteem—their concern was survival and security, pure and simple.[5] With the rise of labor unions and

[5]For a depiction of workers struggling to stay alive in early industrial America read Upton Sinclair's novel *The Jungle*.

social legislation, however, plus four decades of unprecedented prosperity, working conditions changed. Labor won better wages and job security. Many workers found their physiological and safety needs were satisfied—*and a satisfied need ceases to motivate an individual.* These workers began looking to different kinds of satisfactions, satisfactions connected with needs higher on the Maslow hierarchy— the needs for social interaction, esteem, and self-fulfillment. This quest continues into the 1980s. Of course, should economic conditions take a dramatic downturn to a point where survival or job security once again becomes a meaningful concern, then (as Maslow predicted) we can expect many workers to again be motivated by physiological and safety needs.

HOW CAN I IDENTIFY MY OWN WORKERS' NEEDS?

In general, when it comes to today's workers you can be fairly certain (all things being equal) that most of your full-time employees will be striving to fulfill higher-level needs on the Maslow hierarchy.

Of course, there will always be exceptions to any general rule; and for that reason your ability to assess accurately any *specific* worker's needs will be improved if you get to know your employees individually and any personal circumstances that might affect their needs (see Chapter 6, pp. 72–73). For example, those who might normally be concerned with self-esteem will focus instead on security needs if they suddenly finds their financial nest egg destroyed by an unexpected (and costly) medical problem.

Sometimes the only way to be sure about the particular needs of individual workers is to offer them several different on-the-job *rewards,* each designed to satisfy a different need on the Maslow hierarchy, and then watch to see which is the most effective. To do this successfully you'll want to learn more about which rewards go with which needs and how you can administer those rewards effectively in the workplace. This involves the use of behavior modification—a technique you can learn to use once you read Chapters 6, 7, and 8.

Chapter 6

Give the Nod to Behavior Mod

Behavior modification isn't magic, but it sure works like it on the job.

Manager of a fast-food restaurant

You can't satisfy worker needs if you don't know what they are. In Chapter 5 we found out what they are, and now we're ready to satisfy those needs through the use of *behavior modification,* a powerful and exciting behavioral science technique that can be used to fulfill worker needs and enhance worker productivity at the same time.

WHAT IS BEHAVIOR MODIFICATION?

Behavior modification is a *scientific* procedure for systematically changing behavior through the use of rewards or punishments or both. Defined in such a manner, free of academic jargon, the method seems, to some people, to offer nothing new. In one sense, those people are correct: The man who purchases flowers for his wife or spanks his child is practicing a rudimentary form of behavior modification (rudimentary in comparison with the more sophisticated, systematic, and effective behavior modification used by scientists). Nevertheless, these people are incorrect in assuming that behavior modification is "old hat." What makes the approach novel (and effective) is the use of psychological learning principles in the reinforcement of behavior.

Although the major thrust of behavior modification only began in the 1960s, the impetus for the movement came from investigations in the earlier decades of this century. One classic and influential study was performed in 1920 by John Watson, father of psychological behaviorism and advocate of human behavior control. Watson was convinced that such control was feasible and, not one to hide his convictions, once boasted:

> Give me a dozen healthy infants, well formed, and my own specified world to bring them up in and I'll guarantee to take any one at random and train him to become any type of specialist I might select—doctor, lawyer, artist, merchant-chief, and, yes, even beggar-man and thief, regardless of his talents, penchants, tendencies, abilities, vocations, and race of his ancestors.[1]

Unlike many of his contemporaries who speculated on such matters but went no further, Watson set out to substantiate his claims in the laboratory. His proof was gathered at the expense of Albert, a normal, healthy infant. Albert was basically stolid and unemotional. He cried infrequently, didn't scare easily, and, except when confronted with loud sounds, showed no signs of fear. At 9 months of age, he was suddenly presented with objects he had never seen before, including a white rat, a rabbit, a dog, a monkey, cotton, and wool; and he approached these objects without apprehension.

At this juncture, Watson set out to prove his point: that he could control Albert's behavior at will and, specifically, make him afraid of the white rat he now approached fearlessly. The animal was admitted into Albert's playroom, as it had been before, but now each time the

[1]John Watson, *Behaviorism*, People's Institute, New York, 1924, p. 82.

child reached for the animal, a loud gong was struck nearby. After a very few of these encounters, Albert began to cry and scurry away whenever he saw the rat, even when the gong did *not* sound. Furthermore, the child showed fear of other objects that looked like a rat, for example, the white rabbit he had earlier approached without fear. By a few pairings of a negative reinforcer (loud sound) with an initially attractive plaything, Watson was effectively able to condition little Albert's behavior and make him afraid of a whole class of objects similar to and including a white rat.[2]

My First Experience with Behavior Modification

I've always had an "I'm from Missouri . . . show me" attitude about things, so when I first heard about behavior modification as an undergraduate, my first reaction was skepticism. My second reaction was to test it and see what would happen. I was a psychology major and I remember thinking: If this really works, it should work for me. I checked with some of my classmates. They felt the same way. So, in the true spirit of science, we set out to see whether we could control human actions using behavior modification. Our little experiment was conducted on a particularly unpopular teacher, a chap we dubbed Mr. Monotone.

Mr. Monotone was the kind of instructor whose lectures should have been recorded and sold to hardcore insomniacs. I am sure the cure rate would have been astounding. Three times a week, an hour a day, he gave his dreadful little lectures, delivered in a dronelike monotone from a mouth that hardly seemed to move. To make matters worse, Mr. Monotone stood rigidly behind the podium and stared straight ahead when he spoke. In fact, the only real evidence that he was alive (besides the steady stream of words tumbling colorlessly from his lips) was his tendency to scratch his head with his left hand. This little gesture occurred five or six times an hour, usually at 8- to 10-minute intervals.

We decided to see if we could increase the frequency of Mr. Monotone's head-scratching gesture through behavior modification. First we enlisted the aid of a few students in his class (in addition to ourselves) to participate in the "investigation." Once everyone knew

[2]John Watson and R. Rayner, "Conditioned Emotional Reactions," *Journal of Experimental Psychology,* vol. 3, 1920, pp. 1–14.

what to do, we situated ourselves in a row near the front of the class, and here's what we did: Every time Mr. Monotone lectured in his normal, motionless manner we showed no real interest in the lecture. But whenever he made his head-scratching gesture we immediately went into action, nodding our heads in approval, smiling, furiously scribbling notes—everything we could to reward Mr. Monotone with something we figured he needed: social approval.

Sure enough, in a matter of hours, Mr. Monotone was scratching his head like a dog with fleas. Not only did he scratch more frequently, but his hand stayed in his hair longer each time he did.

The results of our little study spoke well for the power of behavior modification to control certain kinds of behavior. It took only a few lectures before Mr. Monotone had increased his head scratching in response to our reward of social approval. Furthermore, when we ended the experiment (stopped giving approval for the head-scratching behavior), it gradually returned to its normal prereinforcement levels.

Little Albert and Mr. Monotone Compared

John Watson's experiment with little Albert and our investigation with Mr. Monotone share one important characteristic: the use of *reinforcement* to change behavior. Behavior modification works by increasing or decreasing the likelihood of a specified behavioral response through systematic reward and punishment. Little Albert received negative reinforcement (loud sound), and it is assumed that such punishment will eventually lead to cessation of the negatively reinforced behavior. In the case of Mr. Monotone, the reinforcement was positive (social approval), and it is expected that rewarded behavior will be maintained (and often increase in frequency). The process by which reinforcement becomes associated with certain behaviors is called *conditioning*. The psychologist uses his knowledge of conditioning principles to make his efforts more effective.

One can get a feeling for the power of conditioning procedures, for how such methods can systematically change a wide variety of human actions, by reading B. F. Skinner's novel *Walden Two*. Although it is labeled a work of fiction, it is grounded in scientific facts, using the established learning principles underlying behavior modification to regulate human behavior and create a utopian community. In reality, the book is a reflection of Skinner's scientific thinking from start to finish, an application of his operant conditioning methods to the design of a society created and governed by psychologists.

In *Walden Two*, everyone is well-behaved, happy, and productive. Citizens are controlled, but they are not aware of being controlled. Control is achieved by procedures similar to those employed by Watson with little Albert and the undergraduates with Mr. Monotone. Explains the novel's psychologist-hero: "When he behaves as we want him to behave, we simply create a situation he likes, or remove one he doesn't like. As a result, the probability that he will behave that way again goes up, which is what we want. Technically it's called 'positive reinforcement.' "[3] *Walden Two* is deeply grounded in the principles of behavior modification.

In the years since the early work of Watson and Skinner, scientists have made behavior modification a far more powerful system for controlling behavior. At the same time, they have used it to change increasingly complex and diverse types of human activity. Some behavior modification takes place in clinical settings, where it is used to eliminate or modify dysfunctional personal behavior. The ability of behavior modification to change entrenched, highly resistant forms of human activity reminds us of its potency as a behavior control device.

USING BEHAVIOR MODIFICATION
IN THE WORKPLACE

It was only a matter of time before the behavior-changing power of behavior modification attracted the attention of the business community. Would the technique be effective in the workplace? Ask Emery Air Freight Corporation. In the early 1970s the company embarked on a pioneering behavior modification program which saved it over $2 million in 3 years.[4]

Part of the program centered on the customer service department, where employees were charged with the responsibility of answering all customer inquiries within a 90-minute time frame. (If you had a question about shipping rates, the goal of the customer service

---

[3]B. Skinner, *Walden Two*, Macmillan, New York, 1948.

[4]Herbert Huebner and Alton Johnson, "Behavior Modification: An Aid in Solving Personnel Problems," *The Personnel Administrator*, October 1974, p. 34.

representative was to get back to you with an answer within 90 minutes.) When customer service representatives were asked how often they met the 90-minute goal, their response was optimistic: 90 percent of the time. Research, however, revealed that the goal was being achieved only 30 percent of the time.

To try and improve employee performance, each customer service representative was asked to record the actual time it took to answer each incoming inquiry on a log sheet. The log sheets were then checked daily by management, and feedback was given to employees concerning how well they were doing. Anytime an employee showed improved performance (more calls answered within the 90-minute limit) they were *rewarded* with praise from their supervisor. Even those who didn't improve their performance received a reward of sorts: they were praised for their honesty and accuracy in filling out their log sheets and were then reminded of the 90-minute goal.

The results of the behavior modification program were dramatic. After a few days of feedback and praise, customer service representatives were meeting the 90-minute time limit 90 percent of the time—and some employees were even setting higher goals for themselves.

The same basic behavior modification design was utilized by Emery Air Freight Corporation in its shipping department. Using the log-sheet approach, shipping department employees monitored their performance and received feedback and praise from their supervisors. The result? Container-packing efficiency jumped from 45 percent to 90 percent, saving the company over half a million dollars per year in shipping costs.[5]

How has the business community reacted to Emery Air Freight's pioneering experience with behavior modification? Being basically conservative, business leaders haven't suddenly embraced the technique as the ultimate cure-all. Yet the developments of the past decade make one thing clear: behavior modification will become an increasingly important management tool for shaping profits and worker satisfaction in the coming years (see Box 6-1). This should come as no

---

[5]Ibid. See also: "New Tool: Reinforcement for Good Work," *Psychology Today,* April 1972, pp. 67–69 (digested from article in *Business Week,* Dec. 18, 1971).

BOX 6-1

PRODUCTIVITY GAINS FROM A PAT ON THE BACK*

When Edward J. Feeney pioneered the systematic use of "positive reinforcement" to cut costs by $2 million . . . at Emery Air Freight Corporation a decade ago, few in the mainstream of management innovation paid much attention. They concentrated instead on other newly evolving techniques, such as job enrichment and management by objectives which seemed easier to implement and freer of dark psychological overtones. Now, though still in an evolutionary stage in business, the Feeney techniques—commonly called "behavior modification" and identified with Harvard psychologist B. F. Skinner—are increasingly being recognized as a valuable tool with which managers can combat slumping productivity growth rates, reduce absenteeism and turnover, and, in most cases, provide increased job satisfaction for employees.

　　Skinner's theories, which hold that all behavior can be affected by positive rewards such as praise or recognition, may seem too obvious to be called a management technique. Indeed, Skinnerians contend, successful managers have always been using behavioral principles, but only now are they attempting to systematize the approach. And many are reporting dramatic results.

　　"A conservative estimate of our cost savings in 1977 alone is $3.5 million, and that is not including employee morale, which is difficult to quantify," says Jay L. Beecroft, who runs a program using Skinner principles at 3M Co. Other major companies adopting such programs, which experts estimate at more than 100, include Frito-Lay, Addressograph-Multigraph, B. F. Goodrich, Weyerhaeuser, and Warner-Lambert. Many are in trial stages, however, or in selected divisions. At 3M, for instance, one program was applied to the specific task of unloading trailers, while at A-M it is being used largely with office workers. Still other companies, such as Ford, American Telephone & Telegraph, and General Electric, are using a modified form of Skinner concepts, incorporating them with other management techniques.

SETTING STANDARDS

Like 3M, most companies using behavior modification have recorded sizable cost savings, along with huge gains in worker productivity. And nearly all have achieved at least a 200% return on investment. In fact, one California firm, Carl Pitts Associates, of Del Mar, guarantees in writing to save companies twice the firm's $15,000 fee in one year.

To structure the approach, successful programs typically begin with a series of meetings in which managers and employees discuss mutual needs and problems and propose solutions. These diagnostic sessions are considered critical because it is in them that managers set standards for job performance and determine how they will be met. At the same time, employees identify their needs and provide their managers with a list of reinforcers that should "modify" the employees' behavior. A-M, for example, holds a three-day session. What workers, such as clerk typists, want most is a sense of belonging, a sense of accomplishment, and a sense of teamwork, says program director C. Eugene Dickerson. In return, managers ask for quicker filing of reports with fewer errors.

The second step is to arrange for worker performance to be observed with a reliable follow-up; the third is to give feedback often, immediately letting employees know how their current level of performance compares with the level desired. At Western Air Lines Inc., for instance, five telephone reservation offices, employing about 1,800 people, keep track of the percentage of calls in which callers make flight reservations. Then they feed back the results daily to each employee. At the same time, supervisors are instructed to praise employees for asking callers for their reservations. Since the program started, the ratio of sales to calls has soared from one in four to one in two.

BONING UP

Contributing to the technique's appeal are a growing number of consultants specializing in the field. Many have jumped into the arena behind Feeney, who set up shop in Ridgefield, Connecticut, in 1974 after his successes at Emery. Behavioral Systems Inc., however, began operating in 1971, and now claims to be the largest in the field, with $2 million a year in business. It employs 35 consultants and is being bankrolled by Minnesota Viking quarterback Fran Tarkenton. Interest has also spread to business schools. At the University of Michigan, for example, reinforcement seminars are constantly overbooked, a turnaround from a couple of years ago. Many companies, such as B. F. Goodrich, are sending managers to class to bone up on the subject. "The organization of the future is learning that productivity can be improved by managing the most important resource, and that is the human resource," says Roger Howe, director of personnel and organizational development at Goodrich, which started using behavior techniques three years ago to reduce scrap costs, among other things.

SUCCESSFUL USERS

Another company that has chalked up good results is Los Angeles–based Collins Foods International Inc., which started a program in 1974 for 70 clerical employees in its accounting staff. After determining the staff's actual performance in such areas as billing error rates, supervisors and employees got together to discuss and set goals for improvement. Employees were praised for reports containing fewer errors than the norm, and results were charted on a regular basis. According to Gerald R. Wahlin, controller, improvements have been dramatic. For instance, the error rate in the accounts payable department fell from more than 8% to less than 0.2%.

Malcolm Warren is another successful user of the technique. He ran behavior modification programs at Questor Corp. and Dayton Hudson Corp. before forming his own company, Performance Technologies Inc., a few months ago, with Saks & Co. among his new clients. While at Dayton Hudson, however, he set up a program to increase sales in the men's department of one of the company's stores. The average sale was $19. Warren established a standard of $25. Employees were taught how to make extra sales and were congratulated by supervisors each time a sale went above $19. Within two months, department sales averaged $23.

With success, quite naturally, comes expansion. At Dallas-based Frito-Lay Inc., a division of PepsiCo. Inc., behavior modification programs are now in place at 23 of 37 plants and soon will be under way at the remainder. Techniques are used only in manufacturing operations, such as the packaging machine assembly line, but the company is looking at applications elsewhere, including sales and distribution. Dr. David A. Lyman, associate manager of management development, stresses that programs must be used carefully, recognizing all the subtle conditions that must accompany them to make them work properly. "Our experience is that we can't go into a plant without some other things occurring first," cautions Lyman. "For instance, in a union plant you have to have an element of trust and cooperation between the personnel manager and union leaders." Another consideration, he says, is the personality of managers. "If you have a bunch of Attila the Huns running the plant, they're more likely to use the system as a club."

GAINING ACCEPTANCE

Lyman also points out that in Frito-Lay plants using behavior modification procedures, the average time required for a first-line supervisor to earn a promotion to a shift manager is 14 to 20 months. And one supervisor, he says, made the jump in nine months. This compares with an average of 24 to 30 months' promotion time in the company's other plants.

This move toward motivating employees to greater productivity is a move in the right direction, but it will be a slow and perhaps painful process for some, warns Kenneth L. Sperling, director of organization and career development at Warner-Lambert Co. The company has been successfully experimenting with Skinnerian principles in packaging operations at plants in Puerto Rico and Mexico, and will be introducing programs at other plants this year. In five or ten years, Sperling says, Skinner principles will be a much more accepted way of doing business. Managers will soon realize that an employee's involvement in determining his own best output level should provide the highest return to the bottom line. "There is a general feeling among managers that Skinner's concepts are undermining what they perceive to be their right to manage," Sperling observes. "But what managers must realize is that managing is not a right, it's a responsibility."

surprise, particularly when you consider the increasing number of psychologists and psychologically trained managers entering the business world. They're familiar with the power of behavior modification, and they'll be in a position to use it on the job. No doubt they will, and I hope you do, too.

INSTITUTIONAL VERSUS PERSONAL BEHAVIOR MODIFICATION PROGRAMS

In reality, there are two kinds of behavior modification programs that can be used in the workplace. One kind I call the *institutional* behavior modification program; it is amply described in Box 6-1. Normally, such a program is a highly formalized, large-scale affair, requiring coordinating and directing skills that come from years of specialized education and training. If as a manager you should be asked to participate in such a program, feel free to do so. But I don't recommend that you *start* one. The responsibility for creating and directing institutional behavior modification programs is best left to professional consultants or in-house organizational development (OD) directors. They have the proper training for the job, you don't.

Do not despair, however. There is still the second kind of program, called the *personal* behavior modification program, that you *can* start; in fact, it is labeled personal because you can use it with your employees even if no other manager in the entire organization follows suit. And, best of all, you don't need the specialized skills of the trained psychologist or professional consultant to make a personal behavior modification program function effectively in the workplace.[6] What you do need is a willingness to commit some time and effort to the undertaking, a caring attitude toward your employees, an unwavering commitment to use behavior modification in an ethical manner and a set of guidelines for applying personal behavior modification on the job. Let us turn to those guidelines now.

HOW YOU CAN UTILIZE BEHAVIOR MODIFICATION WITH YOUR EMPLOYEES

From our discussion of Maslow's need hierarchy and the experiments in behavior modification, you now possess two vital pieces of information:

1 Individual workers have individual needs, and they will behave in ways that lead to the satisfaction of those needs.
2 Behavior that is rewarded will be maintained or will even increase in frequency.

---

[6]This is primarily because personal behavior modification programs (unlike institutional programs) do not present the complex design and coordination problems that require the attention of more highly trained personnel. Let's face it, there are many people who can serve up an excellent feast for ten to twenty guests at home, but that doesn't qualify them to walk into the local restaurant and prepare a banquet for six hundred.

Putting this information together, your goal as a manager is to reinforce appropriate work behavior with rewards that satisfy the particular needs of individual employees. This should enhance worker productivity and satisfy worker needs, thus establishing the ++ relationship essential to making the workplace a worthplace.

To accomplish this goal will require you to successfully complete a three-step process:

Step 1 You will have to identify the specific needs of your individual workers.

Step 2 You will have to satisfy each worker's specific need(s) with the appropriate reward(s).

Step 3 You will have to administer worker rewards effectively.

Step 1, which has already been discussed in Chapter 5, will be examined again in the next few pages.

Step 2 will be discussed in Chapter 7, where you will find the various reinforcements you can use in motivating your workers. You can use any or all of these rewards, depending on your circumstances and the particular needs of your various employees.

Step 3 will be discussed in Chapter 8, where you will learn the basic rules for administering rewards in a manner that maximizes worker productivity and satisfaction.

A FINAL NOTE ON IDENTIFYING WORKER NEEDS

In Chapter 5 I gave you Maslow's behavioral science model to help you understand and identify your workers' needs more accurately. I also pointed out that many workers have the same needs, which tend to cluster on the higher rungs of the Maslow hierarchy. Thus, if you simply assume that *all* your employees have social, esteem and self-actualization needs, you'll probably be right in most instances.

If, however, you want to obtain greater accuracy in identifying your individual workers' needs, then it will be necessary to conscientiously observe them on the job. It doesn't take long to determine a worker's needs once you watch that person in action—in fact, once you have a little observational experience under your belt, you'll be amazed at just how quickly and accurately you can "read" an individual's needs.

Do you want to obtain the *greatest* accuracy in identifying your workers' needs? If so, observe your employees as you give them various rewards. That way you can pinpoint the reinforcements that work best for each employee. Such information is particularly valuable because, in most instances, you'll have to pick from a number of different rewards to use at any given need level of the Maslow hierarchy.

Finally, continue to observe your subordinates even *after* you have ascertained their needs and the rewards they value most. This is crucial, because workers' needs can change over time and so can their attitudes toward particular rewards. For example, some workers get bored with certain rewards if they're used too often, causing them to lose their effectiveness. If you continue to observe your subordinates, you will be alerted to these changes and be able to take corrective action. Otherwise you might miss such changes entirely and wonder why you ended up with a disgruntled, unproductive employee.

It is interesting to note that identifying worker needs with accuracy and practicing effective behavior modification both require the manager to *pay attention to the worker:* to observe, to be aware, to *see* (not look through) the people whom they supervise. I am not exaggerating when I say that paying attention to your employees is a basic prerequisite to becoming an effective human resource manager. Not only does it help you understand your workers, but it motivates them as well—as you shall soon see.

Chapter 7

Fourteen Rewards You Can Use in the Workplace

I feel more like working now that my manager seems to recognize my existence.

Shoe store salesperson

I'd like you to play scientist for a moment and consider what you'd do in the following circumstances.

Here is the situation. A major corporation has called you in to determine if variations in working conditions can influence employee productivity on the job. To find out, you begin by studying illumination in the workplace. Your hypothesis is simple enough: an increase in illumination will lead to an increase in productivity. Your experiment is simple, too. You designate one set of employees the test group and subject it to deliberate changes in illumination while it works; a second set of workers, called the control group, works under the original lighting throughout the experiment. The only problem is that the results are anything but simple; in fact, they are downright perplexing. Here is what you find:

1   Test group productivity rises when illumination is improved (increased)—as predicted by your hypothesis.
2   Test group productivity also rises when illumination is worsened (decreased). (No hypothesis ever predicted that!)
3   Output also increases in the control group—even though illumination remains constant. (Something definitely strange is going on here.)

All right, what do you do? If you answer, "Drop the experiment," you will be doing exactly what *was* done back in 1927 when a group of scientists from the Massachusetts Institute of Technology puzzled over the same results and finally abandoned the project. If, on the other hand, your curiosity is aroused and you decide to investigate further, then you will be doing exactly what was done between 1927 and 1932 by a new team of investigators headed by Elton Mayo, Fritz Roethlisberger, and William Dickson.[1]

Let us assume that you, like the Mayo team, choose to investigate further. You set up a new experiment, this time with a group of employees who assemble telephone relays. You are still concerned with how variations in the working conditions can influence employee productivity on the job. So now you vary several factors and observe what happens. Here is what you discover:

1   You institute rest periods of various durations. Result: Productivity goes up.
2   You provide soup and a sandwich on the job. Result: Productivity goes up.
3   You shorten the workday by an hour. Result: Productivity goes up.

How do you explain your findings? You might reasonably surmise that rest periods, refreshments, and a shorter workday are highly conducive to productivity. If you do, in fact, subscribe to such an

---

[1]E. Mayo, F. Roethlisberger, and W. Dickson, *Management and the Worker,* Harvard University Press, Cambridge, Mass., 1939.

explanation, then you might be a bit hard-pressed to account for this additional experimental finding:

4   For three months all rest periods, refreshments and shortened working days are eliminated, and the employees return to the work schedule they followed before the experiment began. Result: Productivity reaches a new high—and stays there during the entire 12 weeks.

What *is* going on here? And if that's not enough to raise havoc with your scientific theories, consider the final investigative result:

5   Rest periods and refreshments are reintroduced. Result: Output climbs higher still.

O.K., scientist—what's the verdict? It seems that no matter what changes you introduce, worker output increases. Why? Elton Mayo and his associates were faced with the same question over a half century ago when they actually conducted the study with the employees who assembled telephone relays in the Hawthorne Division of the Western Electric Company. They came up with the findings I just described.

How did the Mayo team explain the results? First, they realized that something more than changed working conditions was influencing worker productivity on the job. Then they identified what that "something more" was: the *human dimension*—the social and psychological condition of the employees in the workplace. The results of the Hawthorne studies seemed to indicate that the employees ·were more satisfied and worked harder because Mayo and his associates were *paying attention to them,* making them feel more worthwhile and important on the job. By creating changes in the workplace, the Mayo team was altering the *physical* environment; but more important as far as productivity was concerned, it was also transforming the *psychological* environment by fulfilling the social and personal needs of the workers.

Now, did you guess that it was the human element producing all those strange results at the Hawthorne plant of Western Electric? If you didn't, don't feel bad—neither did Mayo and his colleagues when they first puzzled over their unexpected experimental results. In fact, it took 5 years of experimentation with over 20,000 employee-subjects before they were reasonably sure of what exactly *was* accounting for the increases in productivity.

We all owe a debt of sorts to Mayo and his associates. Even though their work has received some critical brickbats among the bouquets, they were responsible for focusing managerial attention on the human dimension in the workplace. They were also among the first behavioral scientists to recognize that workers can be motivated by social and psychological (as well as economic) needs.

USING REWARDS TO PAY ATTENTION TO THE WORKER

The Mayo team discovered the importance of paying attention to the worker, how it could increase employee output and satisfaction at the same time. Their discovery remains relevant today. In fact, as I pointed out in the previous chapter, paying attention to the worker is basic to determining worker needs and practicing effective behavior modification.

On the following pages I will be discussing fourteen different rewards you can use in satisfying your employees' needs and encouraging their productivity. These rewards are:

1 Praise
   a Job-relevant
   b Non-job-relevant
2 Public recognition
3 Job security
4 Money
5 Fringe benefits
6 Employee development programs
   a Job enrichment
   b Personality (and leadership) development
   c Mental and physical health
7 Employee involvement in decision making
8 Leisure time
9 Feedback
10 Social participation
11 Company spirit (pride)
12 Opportunity to achieve and advance in the organization
13 Degrees of freedom at work
14 Pleasant forms of moderate distraction

Every time you administer a reward you are, in effect, paying attention to the worker; your goal will be to give your subordinates those rewards that best satisfy their particular needs. In other words, you want to achieve a match between workers' needs and the rewards they receive on the job.

Before I turn to a discussion of the various rewards, I will list some points that should help you choose and administer your rewards more effectively. A more complete discussion of these points will be found in Chapter 8.

1   Most of the fourteen rewards are geared to satisfying social, esteem, or self-fulfillment needs. This reflects our thinking that most contemporary workers have needs that fall in the upper ranges of the Maslow hierarchy.

2   The reward that works best is the reward that satisfies a worker's need(s) most successfully.

3   Many workers have several different needs at once, allowing you to use several different kinds of rewards in such circumstances.

4   Certain rewards can satisfy more than one human need. That is, some rewards overlap need levels in the Maslow hierarchy (for instance, money can satisfy physiological, safety, and esteem needs).

5   Certain needs can be satisfied by more than one reward. Choose the reward that works best for the individual worker in question.

6   Be on the lookout for boredom effects if you use the same reward frequently for a particular employee.

7   Don't be afraid to experiment with using the various rewards. The more rewards you can utilize effectively, the better manager you'll be.

REWARD 1: PRAISE

There are two kinds of praise you can use to satisfy worker needs: *job-relevant* praise and *non-job-relevant* praise. Let me discuss each in turn.

Job-Relevant Praise

Complimenting a worker for a job well done is probably the simplest and most basic reward you can administer—and it is also one of the most effective. Remember the survey in Chapter 5? Number 1 on the workers' "want parade" was full appreciation of work done. Praising

an employee for superior job performance can show that appreciation, and unlike some rewards, such as money, it doesn't cost you
anything.

Nationally recognized management consultant Dr. John F. Mee
had this to say when asked if praise pays with today's employees:
"Recognition for a job well-done reinforces an individual's self-image
and self-satisfaction. . . . Praise increases an individual's pride and
. . . hopes of making a contribution. Praise and recognition for a job
well-done make for better employees."[2]

With all the benefits accruing from the use of praise, you'd think
that contemporary managers would use it frequently. Right?

Wrong! Very few managers use praise or use it often enough; in
fact, some are stingier with compliments than Scrooge was with
money. Managers who have this attitude toward praise can usually be
classified into one of two types. If you've ever had a job, you'll
probably think I knew some of the managers you worked for.

Type 1: The Negativistic Manager   This is the type of person
who seems to have mastered the now-you-see-him, now-you-don't
routine. You see him when things go wrong, and you don't when
things go right. Here's how one employee described the behavior of
her negativistic manager:

> I work in sales at a large department store, and my manager has plenty of
> opportunity to observe my performance. On Monday I came to work
> and had a very good morning. My manager said nothing. Monday
> afternoon I sold about normal, and still my manager said nothing. On
> Tuesday I had an exceptional day: I sold way over average. My manager
> said nothing. On Wednesday I had an average sales morning and a good
> afternoon. My manager said nothing. Thursday I got to work a bit early
> for the storewide sale and put in a busy, high-sales day. My manager said
> nothing. Friday started O.K., I sold about normal. My manager said
> nothing. Then at 2:15 Friday afternoon I made a mistake that lost us
> a sale. Bam! The ceiling fell in. From out of nowhere the manager
> came racing up and began hounding me about losing the sale. *All
> I'd like to know is where the hell was she all week long when I was
> doing great?*

---

[2]J. Mee (interview), "Understanding the Attitudes of Today's Employees," *Nation's
Business,* August 1976, p. 24.

The negativistic manager is the person responsible for the often-heard worker lament: The only time my manager talks with me about my work is when I do something wrong. Is it any wonder the worker gripes? The negativistic manager is a real motivation-destroyer. Nobody likes to feel that good work is ignored while any mistake receives maximum management attention. As one worker so aptly told her manager: "At least if you're going to criticize my mistakes, give equal time to my successes."

Type 2: The Perfectionistic Manager   This type of person isn't unwilling to praise a worker for a job well done *as long as the job is done perfectly.* The problem is, the perfectionistic manager's standards are so high that hardly anybody reaches the competence level required to trigger a kind word.

I have had many perfectionistic managers approach me and ask, "Why should I praise workers if they don't measure up to my standard of excellence? Didn't you say that praise should be given only when you think a person honestly deserves it?"

My answers to such inquiries are always the same. Yes, you should only praise a worker when you can do so honestly, but there are ways you can honestly praise a person for work not yet up to your standards while, at the same time, encouraging that person to reach those high standards in the future. Here is what you do. Note the employee's work performance over a period of time. You will see that it varies; that is, sometimes it is better than other times. Now it might be true that even when the worker is performing best, the work might not measure up to your standards; but that shouldn't stop you from congratulating the worker for a better work performance.

There is a difference between saying, "Hey, Ms. Jones, I want to congratulate you on doing better" and "Hey, Ms. Jones, you're doing great work." Possibly, by rewarding a worker for an improvement in work performance you'll encourage that worker to keep improving until reaching, someday, a level a competence that justifies compliments without qualifications. (By the way, rewarding a worker for performance that approaches an ideal standard is called reinforcement by "successive approximations" and is an effective way to increase worker performance and satisfaction on the job.)

Make sure you don't get trapped in the pitfalls of either negativistic or perfectionistic managing when it's your turn to step into a supervisory role. Be prepared to use praise as an effective reward for deserving employees, particularly when those employees have either social or esteem needs, or both.

There are many ways to give praise on the job (see, for example, Box 7-1), but it should always be (1) honest (the employee should deserve the praise), (2) fair (everyone should have an equal chance of getting praise for similar performance), and (3) not so frequent that it loses its effectiveness. When an employee's performance is so great that you feel too much praise might become a problem, then alternate praise with another of the fourteen rewards. That should help reduce the danger of any one reward losing its potency through overuse.

BOX 7-1

THE COMPLIMENTARY INTERVIEW

When most employees think about interviews, they conjure up images of tough-minded corporate recruiters grilling nervous job applicants about their credentials; or else they think about performance appraisals where tough-nosed managers interrogate them about every facet of their job performance. The thought of going through such interviews is not very appealing to most workers; in fact, some find them downright unnerving.

Imagine, then, the pleasant surprise in store for employees who report for interviews with their managers and find out the purpose of the interview is to praise them for their performance on the job. Talk about the intertwining of relief and reward! What these workers have just experienced is the *complimentary interview,* a technique highly recommended by management experts Joseph Cangemi and Jeffrey Claypool.

The complimentary interview is an excellent way to provide deserving workers with praise reward. As the authors observe:

> The complimentary interview program allows management to share respect, praise, concern, trust and appreciation with employees in a formal way. There is evidence that this sort of management/employee communication tends to produce a strong, committed and efficient work force. This approach does not require direct financial investment on the part of the company—only time. On the contrary, even the smallest de-

---

crease in waste, cost or absenteeism, or an increase in safety, production, quality, is a good return on the investment of complimentary interviews.*

*Joseph Cangemi and Jeffrey Claypool, "Complimentary Interviews: A System for Rewarding Outstanding Employees," *Personnel Journal*, February 1978, p. 90.

Non-Job-Relevant Praise

Praise, to be effective, doesn't have to be limited to job performance. People like to be complimented on a whole range of behaviors, and that is where non-job-relevant praise comes in.

Let us presume that you're a manager, and one day you spot a subordinate walking into the office wearing a new outfit. If you honestly think the clothes are attractive, why not compliment the employee for having good taste? Such praise accomplishes two things:

It clearly demonstrates to your employees that you are aware of them (many workers complain that their supervisors don't even know who they are).

1 It satisfies the workers' need for social approval or external validation of their personal worth or for both.

There are many instances in which you as a manager will have the opportunity to practice non-job-relevant praise. For example:

1 Changes in a worker's personal appearance you find suitable for praise

2 Acquisitions by a worker (for instance, a new car, house, briefcase, or watch) you find suitable for praise

3 Significant occasions in a worker's life (for example, birthdays, weddings, graduations)

4 Significant off-the-job achievements in a worker's life (for instance, civic awards, election to office in a social or fraternal organization, religious activities, outstanding performance in sports)

Normally, workers are proud of their non-job-relevant activities, and they will be pleased that you chose to share their pride; however, let me make a few cautionary recommendations:

1   Some workers feel strongly about keeping their work life and personal life separate. Thus, they may feel offended by a manager who invades the privacy of their off-the-job world. This is a relatively rare problem, but one you should keep in mind when giving out non-job-relevant praise.

2   If you are going to congratulate one worker on a special occasion (birthday, graduation, marriage, or other occasion), then you should acknowledge every other worker when similar events occur. The only way you can do this is to gather information from the same source(s) and to be sure to do so regularly.

3   Most workers are pleased to be remembered for positive, happy occasions but might be miffed if a manager was to bring up a negative, I'd-like-to-forget-the-whole-thing event. For example, it would be the height of bad taste for you as a manager to send your employee a note congratulating him for beating a drunken driving rap.

This brings us to a sensitive issue. What should a manager do about an employee's personal tragedy, for instance, a death in the immediate family? There is no general rule I can give you to cover that kind of situation, except possibly to warn you to handle each incident with great tact and care. Under normal circumstances I see no reason why a condolence card cannot be sent, or possibly flowers or a contribution according to the wishes set forth in the obituary. I also feel it is within the bounds of good taste to express your sympathy upon the employee's return to work and your willingness to be of help should any help be desired. An employee will normally appreciate such a considerate gesture and show appreciation in on-the-job performance.

REWARD 2: PUBLIC RECOGNITION

One of my friends is an engineer with an interesting story to tell. It seems that a few years back he was working at a large company that combined public recognition with employee parking in a unique fashion. Here is what happened.

At that particular company parking was a problem, with employee lots strung out a good distance from the main plant. In fact, some of the outlying parking spaces were a 20-minute walk away, which meant that closer-in parking was coveted by all the workers. Then there were the six assigned parking places as close-in as one could get, three on either side of the main plant door, where all employees entered the building. Five of the six slots were reserved for company officers, and each bore the name of the particular executive painted on a large wooden sign. And the sixth space?

It was reserved for the "employee of the month," complete with name painted in bold letters on the parking sign nearby. The benefits of such an honor were clear to the winners: (1) they saved up to 40 minutes a day walking to and from their cars; (2) they got the opportunity to "rub shoulders" with top company officials every day; and (3) all employees walking into the plant saw the name of the employee of the month.

Now that's public recognition! Of course, such recognition doesn't have to be so elaborate to be effective—for instance, simply praising a person in front of others is a form of public recognition that can be very successful. What makes public recognition effective is sharing the news of a worker's meritorious service with others. Individuals with social and esteem needs want the approval of their supervisors and their peers; they want the external validation of their worth that leads to a sense of self-respect and personal pride. And they get it through public recognition.

There are many ways you can give public recognition on the job, some of which you may already be familiar with.

1   Employee of the month. This is one of the most common forms of public recognition and can be utilized for any number of reasons (for example, highest sales, best suggestion, least absentee-ism, highest output, least errors).

2   Secretary for a day. This is normally a promotion sponsored by radio stations. The winner is publicly recognized over the air and often gets a packet of treats (such as dinner and gift certificates) as well. Normally, managers nominate their own secretaries for the contest.

3   Million-dollar round table or similar types of "clubs." Hence, people are publicly recognized for achieving significant sales in a calendar year. Often insurance companies will publish pictures of their million-dollar round-table representatives in a periodical like *Time*. Not only does this reward the employee, it also affords the opportunity to cut the picture out and have it framed for the office, where customers will be duly impressed.

4   Write-ups in the company periodical or the local newspaper.

5 Public praise.

6 Various performance charts or posters showing how an employee is doing on the job. (Sometimes performance charts or posters are used to show sales or other work indices as part of company contests.)

7 Administering honors or awards. Some companies have annual banquets where top employees receive special gifts or praise for superior performances (see Box 8-1).

8 Change in job title.

9 Publicly announced merit raises or bonuses.

10 Bestowing status symbols when appropriate.

The topic of status deserves special mention. There is a whole range of items that can be given to employees for superior performance, some of which are recognized by those employees and their coworkers as *status symbols*. What is recognized as a status symbol can vary from company to company and person to person; yet, some items seem to be almost universally recognized as status-relevant. Normally, we say something is a status symbol when (1) people want it, (2) not everyone can have it, and (3) possession of it gives the owner a degree of prestige.

In the business world there are many generally recognized status symbols, ranging all the way from the old favorite, the executive washroom key, to the ever popular company car, bigger desk, and larger office.[3] Remember almost anything can become a status symbol if it is recognized in those terms by the workers in the company.[4]

[3]Speaking of nicer offices, I had an interesting experience with this type of status symbol at the university. The building where I worked had two kinds of offices: windowed outer offices and windowless inner offices. One of my students pointed out that he thought the more desirable windowed offices were status symbols given out to professors of the highest rank. I checked out the hypothesis, and sure enough, almost every windowed office was occupied by a full professor, whereas the inner offices were assigned to faculty of lower ranks (associate and assistant professors).

[4]Whenever you give a worker some special privilege or equipment be aware that other workers might perceive this as a status symbol—even if you don't intend it that way. A few years ago a telephone company installer was replacing phones in the secretarial pool. The order called for several dozen black phones, one per desk—all in plain view of every other desk in the room. Unfortunately, the installer ended up one black phone short. "No problem," he muttered. He took a yellow phone from the truck and put it on the last desk. By noontime the next day there was almost a general strike by the secretaries who were enraged that one of their colleagues had gotten a yellow phone—a status symbol she didn't "deserve."

Using public recognition as a reward can be very effective in motivating workers and satisfying their needs, particularly if those needs are in the social and esteem range of the Maslow hierarchy. But certain precautions must be taken lest such rewards lead to serious difficulties.

1   When giving public recognition, do it fairly across the board; in other words, don't play favorites. Every employee should have an equal chance to gain public recognition for work performed.

2   Be wary of possible conflict between workers over public recognition. Particularly in small businesses you must be sure that public recognition doesn't stir up jealousies or destructive competitive rivalries between employees.

3   Be concerned if one employee gets a disproportionate share of public recognition. Not only can this lead to distress, frustration, and even "giving up" in other workers; it can also cause public recognition to lose its effectiveness for the recipient when it is overused or, worse, when the recipient shuns it to avoid rejection by the "overlooked" coworkers.

4   Most employees welcome public recognition, but some are shy about being placed in the limelight. If you have a subordinate who feels uncomfortable in the glare of public attention, use other rewards to motivate him.

REWARD 3: JOB SECURITY

As somebody who has battled for academic tenure, the issue of job security is dear to my heart. It's dear to the hearts of labor union representatives, too, and they have repeatedly struggled to gain contractual recognition of job security for workers.

From our earlier discussion it is evident that job security is not the motivator it once was. This is partially due to the fact that many contemporary workers already *have* that security. Then, too, until recently jobs were relatively abundant, and people could find employment if they were willing to look for it. Finally, with the advent of social legislation (for instance, unemployment compensation and welfare) people realized that being out of a job didn't mean being out of a meal. How vital is job security when the unemployed can depend on governmental programs to satisfy their basic needs? (This is particularly true for low-income workers, who can sometimes make more on welfare than on a job.)

Of course, should the economic picture turn bleak (high unemployment, tight money, and so forth), then the reward value of job security will increase once again. Thus your decision to use job security as a reinforcement will hinge, in part, on your reading of current economic conditions. Here are some other factors you'll want to consider when contemplating the use of job security:

1   The reward of job security is most appreciated by individuals who are lower on the Maslow hierarchy, particularly those with *safety* needs.

2   Job security as a reward will be most effective in industries hit hardest by unemployment and economic turmoil (for instance, at the beginning of the 1980s job security became a big issue to workers in the automobile industry).

3   Job security works least effectively for workers who are highly competent or have marketable skills, as they know they will have an easier time finding another job should the need arise.

4   In some companies, job security is already guaranteed in the employment contract, at which point it ceases to be an effective reward.

5   If you satisfy a worker's safety need by giving job security, recognize that new needs will predominate and change your rewards accordingly.

6   The need for job security tends to be highest when people get older (it's not as easy to find another job at an advanced age) and when they experience an upsurge in financial obligations (such as young children and unexpected bills).

REWARD 4: MONEY

With all this talk about workers' "higher needs" and the importance of psychological rewards, some of you might think I'm down on good old-fashioned money as an effective reinforcement. Nothing could be further from the truth. Money is still a very basic consideration in any jobholder's mind, and at least one management authority believes: "Money may not be the only people motivator, but many realists believe it's still the strongest one around. Apart from the material things, money buys education and opportunity, peace of mind, dignity, and more. In large measure, if you know what to do with it, money buys happiness."[5]

The same author recognizes, however, that money is not "the *only* motivator—people respond as well to interesting and meaningful work, humane treatment, or a feeling of importance and belonging."[6] In other words, there's more to life than cash.

When is it best to use money as a motivator on the job? When your employees require it to satisfy either physiological or safety needs or both. In general, workers who have financial hardships (because of unexpected costs, additional expenses, downturns in the economy, or low wages) find money more rewarding than employees who are more financially secure. There is, however, an exception to this rule. Some people equate money with self-worth and attempt to accumulate as much as they can to satisfy their esteem needs. For them, money is always a valuable reward, no matter how much they get.

Money can also be an effective motivator when it is given in a way that satisfies more than one need at a time. For example, a merit raise, publicly announced, can satisfy lower- *and* higher-level needs simultaneously (see Box 7-2).

[5]R. Dreyfack, "Dismal Disincentives," *Management Review,* December 1976, p. 51.
[6]Ibid., p. 49.

BOX 7-2

MONEY FOR MERIT

Many managers believe that money rewards can only be used to satisfy lower-level needs in the Maslow hierarchy. Not so. Money can also satisfy higher-level needs, and sometimes two or more needs at one time. It all depends on how the money is utilized with employees. At Xerox Corporation two cash merit award programs mix money with a dash of public recognition and a sprinkling of personal achievement. The result: a winning recipe for employee satisfaction and productivity.

The first type of merit award, called the Special Merit Program, is given to about 1 percent of the employees for significant contributions to the company. The amount? A lump sum of cash not less than 5 percent or more than 10 percent of the employee's annual salary.

The second type of award, called the President's Award, recognizes only the most outstanding contributions to Xerox. Very few of these awards are given, but for those employees who do receive them, the cash rewards are substantial: from 10 percent to 50 percent of annual base salary. In addition, award recipients are honored in an annual awards ceremony held at corporate headquarters, just the thing to satisfy even the most discriminating esteem need!

This information was reported in *Management Review*, June 1978, p. 44.

Finally, money rewards are often effective with part-time employees, particularly those who don't see their part-time job leading to full-time employment. Part-time employees often take work *specifically* to make money and, lacking any long-term commitment to the job, are not as excited by rewards that appeal to the career needs of full-time employees. It's like the difference one sees between a house renter and a house buyer. The person who buys a house sees it as a long-term investment and takes pride in that investment. A renter, on the other hand, has no such long-term commitment to the house and often treats it differently for that reason.

What are the problems with using money as a reward? There are two basic difficulties:

1 In most cases, if you use it too often or give out too much, it tends to lose some of its reinforcing effectiveness (even a starving person can get too much to eat).

2 Many times your financial resources will be limited, and you won't have funds available to use as rewards. In these circumstances it is imperative that you have other rewards ready for use with your employees.

In summary, money can be an effective reward, but it's not the *only* effective reward, and it shouldn't be used exclusively to increase worker productivity and satisfaction on the job. Remember, man does not live by bread alone.

REWARD 5: FRINGE BENEFITS

There are numerous kinds of fringe benefits employees can receive on the job—and, like money, how they are presented will determine what needs they can fulfill. In general, fringe benefits help satisfy safety (security) needs; but when they are tangible objects like company cars, then they can act as status symbols or a form of public recognition which can lead to satisfaction of esteem needs.

When asked if fringe benefits play a role in motivating workers, management adviser Arthur Witkin had this to say:

> Some recent studies show that fringes, when absent, can serve to demotivate, but when they're present, they aren't a positive motivating force. . . . Many psychologists, including myself, have accepted the fact that there are so-called hygienic factors involved in job satisfaction. If those factors aren't there, the company's in trouble because workers will feel their absence. But to pile on more of them has no noticeable effect in making workers more satisfied or more productive.[7]

This is an interesting point of view and seems to suggest that a certain number of fringe benefits are necessary because employees expect them, but that beyond that number they don't have much motivational impact. The vital question becomes: How *many* fringe benefits does the employee expect? There is no easy answer to this inquiry, as different workers in different industries have different needs and expectations.

In today's business world, most workers have come to expect fringe benefits like vacations, sick leave, and good group health insurance; beyond that, however, you will have to test and see whether additional benefits are worth the cost in terms of increased satisfaction and productivity in your employees.

REWARD 6: EMPLOYEE DEVELOPMENT PROGRAMS

There are three kinds of employee development programs you can use to satisfy worker needs: (1) job enrichment, (2) personality (and

[7]A. Witkin (interview), "How Bosses Get People to Work Harder," *U.S. News & World Report,* Jan. 29, 1979, p. 64.

leadership) development, and (3) mental and physical health. Let me discuss each in turn.

Job Enrichment

Let me introduce this topic with a personal story. A few years ago I was on a promotional tour, appearing on various radio and television programs to discuss a book I had written. Most of these programs were talk shows, involving 10 to 15 minutes of discussion between the host and myself. It was a comfortable, easygoing format. There was one exception, however: somehow I had been scheduled to discuss my book on a morning rock show—the kind with a disc jockey who plays "Top Ten" music to legions of rock fans listening frenetically by their radios. The idea of discussing my book between hit records, weather reports, and local ad spots—all at the hyperspeed preferred by disc jockeys—was a trifle disconcerting, but I knew it would be worth it. You see, most of my youth was spent dreaming about becoming a disc jockey, and now, at last, I was going to meet one face to face.

And I wasn't disappointed—at least, not at first. In fact, I was so fascinated with the disc jockey and his control room antics that I hardly remember the actual program. Afterward he invited me to lunch in the station's cafeteria. I gladly accepted. We ate at a small table by ourselves, and I waited patiently until he was finished before I asked him *the* question.

"Tell me," I asked, "How does it feel?"

He looked at me blankly. "What do you mean?"

"How does it *really* feel to be a disc jockey?"

His expression didn't change.

I decided to elaborate. "I mean, how does it feel to be right in the center of things—with rock stars on the one side, and the fans on the other . . . and you right in the middle of the action?"

The disc jockey—my hero—stared straight ahead with tired eyes and shattered my little illusion with one verbal shot. "It feels boring," he said flatly, "all I want to do is go home and go sailing." And with that he nodded goodbye and walked out of the cafeteria.

I sat stunned for several minutes before I got up and headed for the exit. On my way out I passed an observation window where I could see the afternoon disc jockey spinning records and talking into his microphone. I stopped to watch his frantic activity and then it hit me: Yes, it would be great to be a disc jockey for a while—a year, maybe two—but then how interesting would it be to sit in a little cubicle and tout the local pizza palace while spinning little discs on a turntable and making the weather sound as exciting as the play by play of the superbowl? Not very exciting at all, I decided, and I began to understand what my host had meant about boredom a few minutes before.

You know, boredom is a very important factor in the human condition. It can motivate us to expand our horizons as we seek new kinds of stimulation; yet, it can also be the "rust of human emotion," leading to dissatisfaction with people, jobs, and activities as we become used to them.

Let us consider boredom and its relationship to work. Any job, no matter what kind it is, has the potential to become boring to the jobholder if the job remains basically the same over a long period of time. This is because, as we learn a job, the skills that were once a challenge become automatic, and the things that were novel and exciting when .we started work become mundane and predictable after being repeated day after day.

How *fast* a job becomes boring will vary, depending in part on the complexity of the job, how much the job changes over time, the personality of the employee, and the skills of the manager in keeping the employee satisfied and productive. (I have often heard a worker comment: "I'd quit this boring job if it wasn't for my manager.")

Only recently have behavioral scientists begun to recognize the significance of boredom in affecting worker satisfaction and productivity. To combat this motivation crippler they have come up with an antidote: *job enrichment.* They have studied the effectiveness of this antidote in the workplace, usually on the assembly line type of job, where the repetitive, relatively simple kinds of tasks invite boredom (see Box 7-3).

Do not think, however, that the assembly line is the only place where boredom can strike with devastating results. Remember *any* job can bet boring if a person stays on it long enough and the job doesn't change. And that goes for blue-collar work, white-collar work, unskilled labor, professional work, and—yes—managerial work, too.

BOX 7-3

JOB ENRICHMENT—"AUTO"MATICALLY

When it comes to job enrichment, the automotive industry takes a back seat to no one! Big name automakers like General Motors, Ford Motor Company, and Volvo have already implemented job enrichment programs on their assembly lines as a way to combat boredom and increase worker satisfaction and productivity. For example, at Volvo's new automobile assembly plant workers can listen to popular music, choose to work in teams, and even read a book or go for coffee while waiting for additional work. At some General Motors plants employee opinions are actively solicited by management. Workers are asked how they would go about solving various defect problems that arise during car assembly. Says John Mollica, assistant director for labor relations, "We try for an interchange of ideas and principles—something more than a boss-employee relationship—in order to involve the worker."

The job enrichment experiences of the major automakers has encouraged other industry groups to get involved in the approach—an approach you might find profitable to use in your workplace. For more information on job enrichment and how it is used, see the references listed below.

- "Big Firms Start to Talk Job Enrichment," *Industry Week,* July 9, 1973, pp. 42–46.
- B. Northrup, "Working Happier: More Swedish Firms Attempt to 'Enrich' Production-Line Jobs," *The Wall Street Journal,* Friday, Oct. 25, 1974.
- R. Schrank, "How to Relieve Worker Boredom," *Psychology Today,* July 1978, pp. 79–80.
- J. Robins, "Firms Try Newer Way to Slash Absenteeism as Carrot and Stick Fail. More Try 'Job Enrichment,' Seeking to Raise Morale; A Box Plant Gets Results. All 'Cures' Seem Temporary," *The Wall Street Journal,* March 14, 1979, p. 1ff.

As a manager what can you do about boredom? How can you combat this potentially destructive factor and keep worker satisfaction and productivity high? By utilizing job enrichment when possible—that is, when your efforts are allowed by upper management and existing contractual obligations.[8] Here are two objectives you'll want to accomplish in overcoming boredom.

Objective 1: Identify Bored Workers   Not all workers are bored with their jobs. You'll have to determine which ones are bored before you can take corrective action. (Trying to modify the work conditions of a person who is *not* bored on the job can create a terrible hassle.) If a worker has been assigned a specific job for a long time, and if that job is relatively easy for that particular worker to master, then the possibility of boredom increases. Watch for telltale signs, such as listlessness and lack of interest at work, increasing complaints and absenteeism, and loss of morale and productivity. Of course, these signs can also be indications of problems other than boredom—and if they remain after Objective 2 is attempted, then you'll want to look for other causes of the worker's dissatisfaction.

Objective 2: Help Workers Overcome Their Boredom through Job Enrichment   There are several ways you as a manager can help workers enrich their work world. The best way is to expand job responsibilities at a rate which keeps the employee challenged but not overwhelmed. Thus, as a person masters job skills, additional or different ones are assigned. Sometimes this means expanding a specific job to include new responsibilities and skills; other times it means promoting an employee to a new job "up the line." In either case, the emphasis is on giving the employee job enrichment to maintain interest and fend off boredom in the workplace.

"But," some of you may be asking, "what if an employee doesn't want new responsibilities? What if that person is happy the way things are?"

These are reasonable questions and deserve careful answers. Let me deal with the second question first: If the worker *is* happy the way things are, then my recommendation is to "let sleeping dogs lie"— don't tamper with an employee's job if he likes it the way it is. Normally, happy workers are *not* bored workers; they are usually

---

[8]Sometimes upper management or the employee contract (or both) very specifically limits the degree to which a job can be expanded. Be sure you know how much you can change a person's job before you start a job enrichment program with your employees.

interested, satisfied, and productive in the workplace—which means that you, the manager, will have reason to be happy, too.

Now, for the first question, there will probably be some workers who are bored and do not want new or additional responsibilities. You will have to use your best judgment as to whether forcing changes on these workers will later be met with a "Thank you, I wish you had done that earlier" or with even greater dissatisfaction on the job. Fortunately, you won't have to make this judgment very often, because in most cases bored workers welcome a chance to get out of their rut into work that is more challenging and stimulating.

Boredom is not an enjoyable human condition—people normally strive to avoid or eliminate it. If you can help them in their quest, all the better for you and for the worker. Just make sure that the workers don't feel you're ripping them off in the process. A worker who can readily take on new job challenges as a means of overcoming boredom may pass up the chance completely if that worker senses the manager is merely trying to get more work without paying for it. The best way to approach the idea of job enrichment, then, is in a voluntary context—giving the worker the option to accept or reject the job opportunities. That way, the employee will see the offer in the positive way it was intended, rather than as simply another attempt to get more work at no extra pay.

There are numerous job enrichment programs you can utilize with your employees (see, for example, the ones discussed in Box 7-3). Some require additional education or training programs, which in themselves help combat boredom.[9] Here are some job enrichment approaches you can use to help combat boredom on the job. Whichever ones you choose should be adapted to your particular work circumstances for maximum effectiveness.

1   On some jobs (for instance, on assembly lines) it is possible to rotate workers through several types of jobs, thus relieving the boredom of doing the same task time after time.

2   You can continually expand a person's job to encompass new skills and responsibilities.

3   You can promote an individual to a new job that may be more demanding.

[9]See, for example, J. Velghe and G. Cockrell, "What Makes Johnny Mop," *Personnel Journal*, June 1975, pp. 324ff.

4   You can change a person's working environment, to keep it novel and stimulating (see Reward 14).

5   You can let the worker get involved in team production efforts (see Reward 10).

6   You can give the worker more "degrees of freedom" in controlling the job (see Reward 13).

7   You can let the worker participate in the managerial decision-making process (see Reward 7).

Before moving on to the other forms of employee development programs, let me make one final point about job enrichment.

It is sometimes tempting to look at certain kinds of jobs—particularly repetitive ones like those on assembly lines—and automatically label them boring. This is a bad mistake you shouldn't make. A job that seems boring to one person might be perfectly satisfying and even highly challenging to someone else; it will depend to a great degree on the ability of the person to perform the task in question. There are always some individuals who enjoy doing the very jobs that others would find boring the minute they walk in the door.

As a manager, you should be striving for successful job-worker matches—in other words, jobs that fit the needs of the individual workers performing them. In doing this, don't ask yourself, "Would I find this job boring?"; ask yourself, rather, "Would my employee find this job boring?" After all, it's the worker who is going to have to do the work.

Personality (and Leadership) Development

Almost all major corporations and many smaller businesses offer their employees the opportunity to attend various seminars and workshops designed to improve job performance through the development of personal strengths (for example, creativity development, and assertiveness training). These programs can run from a few hours to a full week of intensive "marathon" sessions, and they are normally conducted by in-house specialists (usually the organizational development staff) or outside consultants hired for training purposes.

Because personality and leadership development programs normally require the direction of specialists, you probably won't be called upon to conduct any workshops unless you've had specialized training to do so. Therefore, I simply call these programs to your attention as another approach to improving worker satisfaction and productivity on the job. If your particular company doesn't have such programs, you might want to recommend their implementation—if you think they would be of value in your particular work environment.

Mental and Physical Health Programs

American business is waking to the profound personal and financial waste that occurs when a valued employee is mentally or physically incapacitated at the height of a productive career. In many cases, such mental or physical breakdowns could have been prevented had the proper preventative steps been taken. Major American corporations are now committed to developing programs to help safeguard the health and mental well-being of their employees. For example, corporations like Exxon, Mobil Oil, and General Motors are beginning to implement "executive fitness" programs in an attempt to lessen dramatically the risk of premature death among their executives. The investment of time and money is well spent. As William DeCarlo, manager of recreation services for Xerox Corporation, observes: "The death of a top executive means loss of what is stored in his mind. If we can prevent one fatal heart attack, we will have paid for our physical fitness program for several years."[10]

Good mental and physical fitness is vital to employee satisfaction and productivity on the job. And this applies to *all* employees—managers as well as their subordinates. A full discussion of this topic will be found in Section 3: *"How to succeed in business without really dying."*

All three employee development programs share a common characteristic—they are rewarding because they make workers' feel better about themselves. This "feeling better" can take many forms. Sometimes a worker feels more enthusiastic and less bored with life (job enrichment), other times more self-confident (personality development) or robust and alert (physical health). Whatever form it takes, however, can be rewarding to the individual, and for that reason employee development programs provide an effective method for increasing worker satisfaction and productivity on the job.

[10]W. DeCarlo, personal communication, 1977.

REWARD 7: EMPLOYEE INVOLVEMENT IN
DECISION MAKING

The following incident took place many years ago in a company that manufactured wooden toys. One part of the process consisted of spraying paint on partially assembled toys, and then hanging them on an overhead belt of continuously moving hooks which carried the toys into a drying oven. The eight employees who did the painting sat in a line in front of the hooks. The plant engineers had calculated the speed of the belt so that a trained employee would be able to hang a freshly painted toy on each hook before it passed out of reach. The employees were paid on a piece rate basis, determined by their performance as a group. New employees were put on a learning bonus, which decreased every month. At the end of 6 months, the learning bonus was cut off and the employees were on their own.

The painting operation was a management headache. High turnover, low morale, and frequent absenteeism were the symptoms. The employees complained that the hooks were moving too fast and that the time study engineers had set the piece rates wrong. Many of the hooks were moving into the oven without toys on them.

A consultant was hired by the plant management to study the situation. After preliminary investigation, the consultant tried several times to persuade the supervisor to call a meeting of the toy painters to discuss working conditions with them. The reluctant supervisor finally agreed, and the first of several meetings was held right after the end of a shift. At the meeting a spokesperson for the employees elaborated on their complaints about the speed of the hooks. She explained that they could keep up with the moving hooks for short periods of time but purposely held back for fear that they would be expected to maintain the pace all day long. What they wanted was to "adjust the speed of the belt faster or slower, depending on how we feel." The supervisor agreed to pass this request along to the engineers and superintendent.

As might be expected, the engineers reacted unfavorably to the proposal, and only after much persuasion did they agree to try out the idea. The supervisor had a graduated control dial with points marked low, medium, and fast installed at the booth of one of the employees. The speed of the belt could now be adjusted within these limits.

What happened? The toy painters were delighted with this arrangement and spent much of their free time during the first few days deciding how the speed of the belt should be varied from time to time during the day. Within a week the pattern had been established. The productivity of the group as well as their morale went up considerably. The quality of their work was as satisfactory as it had been previously. And it is interesting to note that the average speed at which the toy painters were running the belt was *higher* than the constant speed they had been complaining about to the supervisor.[11]

For our purposes, the true story of the toy painters illustrates an extremely important principle for effective managing. If you want to increase worker satisfaction and productivity on the job, then involve your employees in the managerial decision-making process (see Box 7-4).

[11]Reported in W. Whyte, *Money and Motivation*, Harper, New York, 1955.

BOX 7-4

GUESS WHO'S COMING TO DINNER

It's not your ordinary business lunch. Joe and Mary from purchasing are there. So are Diane, Sue, and Steve from the accounting department. Cynthia is there too, along with two other secretaries from the central office. Not an executive in the bunch, clerical workers all. Why, then, are they eating with the president of the corporation?

Because the president wants to talk with them about the company. He wants to listen to their gripes and note their suggestions. He wants to examine their feelings about company issues and give them a chance to ask questions about company actions that affect them. In short, he wants to get rank and file involvement in decision making; he wants to encourage employees to add their voice to company policy.

This face-to-face approach by upper management to discover what is on the minds of the rank and file is called *deep sensing* and has two potential benefits:

1 *It can increase worker satisfaction and productivity.* Many executives who have utilized deep sensing report an across-the-board boost in employee morale. Workers feel that someone "up there" cares about them and is giving them a chance to participate in the creation of the policies that will affect their lives. One clerical worker put it this way: "I feel I'm heard now, that I'm not just a number."

2 *It can bring to upper management's attention useful employee ideas that might otherwise go unnoticed.* For instance, ". . . Shell Canada . . . has been holding meetings to 'sense' employee feelings on specific issues such as career planning and cost reduction. Marjorie Blackhurst, employee communications manager, says that the 600 employees involved in the sessions turned up ideas that yielded the company more than $1 million in savings."*

Deep sensing is one way managers involve their employees in the decision-making process. There are other ways as well, and skillful managers will want to use the approach that works best with their particular employees.

Here are some other articles on employee involvement in decision making that you might find interesting:

- "Participative Management, Bonuses Boost Productivity for Michigan Firm," *Commerce Today,* Nov. 11, 1974, pp. 12–13.
- D. Curley, "Employee Sounding Boards: Answering the Participative Need," *The Personnel Administrator,* May 1978, pp. 69ff.
- J. Donnelly, "Participative Management at Work," *Harvard Business Review,* January-February 1977, pp. 117–127.
- E. Lawler, "Workers Can Set Their Own Wages Responsibly," *Psychology Today,* February 1977, pp. 109–112.
- M. Ways, "The American Kind of Worker Participation," *Fortune,* October 1976, pp. 168ff.

*From "Deep Sensing: A Pipeline to Employee Morale," *Business Week,* Jan. 29, 1979, p. 126.

In the toy factory, the employees were given the opportunity to become involved in the decision-making process. They made recommendations about how the conveyor belt should move, and those recommendations were followed. What happened? Worker satisfaction and productivity increased.

The toy factory results are not unique. In fact, the value of employee involvement in decision making (also referred to as "participative management" in some circles) is one of the most documented and replicated findings in all behavioral science.

By involving your employees in the decision-making process, three benefits can result:

1 Workers who play an active role in the decision-making process will be more likely to go along with whatever decision is reached.
2 Workers who play an active role in the decision-making process will carry out those decisions in a more enthusiastic, motivated manner.
3 By involving your workers in the decision-making process you increase your chances of finding the best possible solution to any given problem. (This is because an employee may come up with a solution which is better than any you were able to devise.)

Many contemporary managers balk at the suggestion that they involve their workers in the decision-making process. They usually base their opposition on arguments that fall apart when held up to close scrutiny. Let me present these arguments and reveal why you as a manager don't have to worry about them if you decide to use employee involvement in decision making as a reward in the workplace.

Argument 1   I can't let my employees share in decision making because they might come up with a recommendation I can't live with.
My Response   Involving employees in the decision-making process doesn't mean that you have to accept every recommendation they make. There are times when your employees will come up with the same recommendation you favor or with a suggestion that you think is better than your own. In such cases you can use their inputs. Other times they won't have any ideas on the problem or their suggestions will be unacceptable (or inferior to your own). In those cases, thank your subordinates for their assistance and go with your own best suggestion.
Argument 2   I can't let my employees share in decision making because if I reject their recommendations they'll become frustrated and demotivated on the job.
My Response   Not necessarily so. If you consistently ask employees for their suggestions and never use any of them, or if you accept employee suggestions on minor issues and ignore them on every major problem that comes along, then you might have a problem with employee morale. On the other hand, no employees expect a manager to accept every suggestion they make; in fact, they

might question your managerial competence if you did. As long as your subordinates feel you are asking for their help in good faith—accepting suggestions which are appropriate and rejecting those which are not—you'll be in good shape.

Argument 3 I don't want to involve my employees in decision making, because then I'll have to check with them every time a problem comes up.

My Response This isn't true. You can involve your employees in decision making as often or as little as you want. There will be some times and problems where soliciting employee inputs will be irrelevant or inappropriate. Also, situations will arise where there is not time to consult with subordinates or where subordinates have no desire to be involved in the decision-making process. Don't let such instances hassle you. Involve your employees when you think it will increase their satisfaction and productivity on the job.

Argument 4 I don't want to involve my employees in decision making because they aren't capable of making decisions.

My Response Often employees are more capable of assisting in decision making than managers realize. This is not because they are brighter than managers, but, rather, because they can bring different perspectives to bear on the problem in question. Let me give you an example. During World War II, an Allied airbase in the Pacific was having supply problems. One item in short supply was protective glass encasements for the landing lights. The ranking officer on the base was at a loss to solve the problem, so he decided to solicit recommendations from base personnel. Within a few hours the problem was solved. A cook in the mess hall, hearing of the problem, quickly realized that empty peanut butter jars would fit perfectly over the landing lights. Not only did the jars fit as well as the original encasements, but they were also stronger and withstood more pounding before breaking. Who would have figured a cook could solve a problem a base commander couldn't crack? The reason he could was that he brought a different perspective to the problem. He worked with peanut butter jars every day, the commanding officer did not. Remember, don't sell your employees short when it comes to giving aid in problem solving. More and more companies are realizing that when it comes to solving work problems, who should know better than the people who do the work (see Boxes 7-3 and 7-4).

Argument 5 I can't let my employees share in decision making because decision making is my job as a manager.

My Response It is your job to make decisions, but that doesn't mean you can't have help. Remember, by involving your employees in the decision-making process you gain additional input for solving the problem. You also create more motivated, satisfied, and productive workers—and that's your job as a manager, too.

Argument 6   I can't let my employees share in decision making because they'll think I'm incompetent and can't solve problems on my own.

My Response   If you sat quietly by and let your employees solve every problem that came along, maybe this would be a possibility. If, however, you get actively involved in the decision-making process, sharing your ideas with your employees and vice versa, then you will not be seen as incompetent but, rather, a concerned manager who values what your employees have to say.

Argument 7   I can't let my employees share in decision making because if I accept their recommendation and it turns out badly, I'll be held responsible for it.

My Response   It is true that you will be held responsible for any bad decision made, whether it be your own or that of your subordinates. But why should this cause any special difficulties? You simply don't accept poor decisions, whether they be yours or your subordinates.

When you add up all the arguments and counter-arguments, one simple conclusion stands clear: Managers have much more to gain than lose by involving their subordinates in the decision-making process. Workers like to feel they have a say in their destiny, that they are "in on things" and can claim some ownership of the policies that affect their lives. That's the way employees are, and refusing to accept them as they are isn't going to change them—it will simply frustrate and demotivate them. When it comes to giving out rewards in the workplace, don't forget the value of involving your employees in the decision-making process.

REWARD 8: LEISURE TIME

Item   A worker in Wisconsin decides to share his job with another employee. His pay is cut in half, but he explains, "I want more time to fool around with my tenor sax."[12]

---

[12]Quoted in K. Sawyer, "Work Habits in U.S. Changing," *St. Petersburg Times,* Jan. 1, 1978, p. 1-A.

Item   A certified public accountant limits her practice so that she has time to write the great American novel.

Item   A husband and wife both cut their working hours so that they can spend more time at home with their family.

Item   A successful salesman takes a whopping cut in commissions so that he can have ample opportunity to fish and hunt.

The salesman, the husband and wife, the accountant, the Wisconsin employee—all have one thing in common: they want to cut their working hours so that they'll have more time to do other things. And they're willing to take a corresponding cut in pay to get their wish. "People say time is money; well, I say less money is more time," is the way one worker explained it.

Such attitudes should come as no surprise. As I indicated earlier, as workers have found their basic needs satisfied, they have developed other, higher level needs—and the need for *leisure time* is one such need.

There are several ways that you as a manager can take advantage of this need for leisure time and use it to create greater worker satisfaction and productivity on the job. It involves using leisure time as a reward. Let me give you two examples of how this can be done.

Tactic 1: Leisure Time Tied to Production Rate   With this tactic, employees are free to leave the workplace once they have produced a specified number of products or completed a defined amount of work. As an example, let's assume you manage a group of employees who produce wickets for the international market. Let us assume further that ten wickets is the daily acceptable production output per worker. Using the leisure-time-tied-to-production-rate tactic, you allow employees to leave the workplace once they have produced their ten wickets. Thus an employee who has worked diligently can leave early and gain more leisure time. Of course, the quality of wicket production has to remain satisfactory—and to make sure it does, you will probably want to institute a quality control check to maintain standards.

Tactic 2: Redistribution of Working Hours   This tactic allows you to give workers more leisure time by rearranging work hours rather than reducing time.[13] You determine an acceptable number of hours per week a worker should be on the job; then you let the individual employees determine when each will put in those hours. Of course, this tactic can only be utilized in situations where hours can be shifted without a deleterious effect on the business.

Here is an example of how Tactic 2 might be utilized in the workplace. Let us assume you are a manager in a company where the following conditions exist: (1) your subordinates currently work a 40-hour week: 8 hours a day, 5 days a week; (2) their work is the kind that can be conducted in a 4-day workweek without any loss in profits; and (3) it is also the kind of work that can be done, without additional personal risk or loss in quality, for 10 hours a day. If these three conditions exist, you meet with your subordinates and give them the choice of working four 10-hour days or five 8-hour days per week. If your workers favor the 4-day week and the accompanying 3-day weekend, then you have just established a ++ relationship. Your employees get a redistribution of working hours they find more to their liking (employee goal); and you still get 40 hours of work from your subordinates (management goal). Everybody wins, nobody loses. And that's what good management is all about.

This redistribution-of-time tactic can also be used to set starting and stopping hours for daily work. For instance, some employees might hate coming to work at 8 A.M. but would be very glad to stay at work until 7 P.M. Why not let them come in at 10 A.M. and work until 7 P.M. Again, assuming their work won't be affected by the different hours, this might be a viable way to satisfy a worker's special time needs and still get the required number of work hours.

In today's energy-conscious world, the redistribution of time is becoming increasingly popular. Already the rigid, fixed-hour work-week is giving way to more flexible time spans based on individual company and employee requirements. This new development is called "flextime" in the literature, and don't be surprised if you see a lot more of it in the years to come. This is as it should be. As one politician wisely observed: "The standard 40-hour workweek has been a sacred cow since the depression. Well, we have different

---

[13]Technically, you are not really giving workers more leisure time by rearranging work hours, but *psychologically* it seems that way to the worker, and that's what counts.

problems now.''[14] One of those problems is the present-day worker who has a need for more leisure time. When you use time as a reward, you'll be able to satisfy that need and get more productive employees in the bargain.

REWARD 9: FEEDBACK

I'd like you to stop for a moment, close your eyes, and try to re-create in your memory several recent cartoons you have seen that deal with business people. Try to re-create as much of each cartoon as you can remember. Now—did you notice any similarities among the cartoons? Any common elements? Let me suggest one: the business chart. In almost every business cartoon I've seen, particularly those featuring a business manager, there is a performance chart in the scene. It may be on the back wall of the office, on a desk, or maybe on an easel or blackboard—but somewhere there is a business performance chart, jagged lines and all.

It's no accident that the business manager and the business chart have been linked in the cartoonist's art and the public's eye. To business managers, *knowledge of how they are doing* is very important—and the business chart is one way that knowledge is recorded and displayed.

This brings us to the topic of *feedback*. Feedback is knowledge of results—information that lets us know how well we're doing at a specific task. Here's an example. Imagine you are visiting your first English pub and your host challenges you to a game of darts. Never having played, you graciously decline and then—in the finest American spirit—run out, buy a set, and begin practicing in your hotel. After the first hundred tosses you begin getting a feel for the game; by the next day, you're ready to go out and challenge the Queen's finest.

You have learned your dart game well. But let us pretend you were forced to practice your throws blindfolded and with plugs in your ears. Could you ever perfect your toss under these conditions? No. Improvement would be impossible because you lacked the vital component of learning: feedback concerning your performance.

[14]Quoted in Sawyer, op. cit., p. 12-A.

Deprived of visual feedback—unable to gain knowledge of the results of your dart throwing—your plight would be hopeless.

We use feedback so regularly in our everyday life that we seldom realize how pervasive and important it is. Yet as one eminent scholar has pointed out: "Every animal is a self-regulating system owing its existence, its stability and most of its behavior to feedback controls."[15] It is only when we are suddenly deprived of our normal opportunity to receive feedback—for instance, in the case of sudden blindness—that we come to understand its momentous value for our very survival.

Because feedback is essential for improving performance, one would think it would be used extensively in the business world. Sadly, most managers don't even come close to providing their employees with adequate knowledge of results to maximize effective performance. And what makes this doubly tragic is that feedback, for many employees, is more than simply a way to improve performance, it is also a *reward* that can satisfy personal needs and lead to greater satisfaction and productivity in the workplace. In other words, workers need feedback to improve their performance, and they want feedback to know how they're doing. The need to know is deeply ingrained in the human character, and particularly in the character of the business manager. Managers have their business performance charts on the wall—why shouldn't subordinates have feedback, too?

In a very informative article, Professor Robert Kreitner identifies three different kinds of feedback you can give your employees to help bolster their satisfaction and productivity in the workplace.

Types of Feedback

1 Informational Feedback This type of feedback helps employees find out how well they are performing on the job. For example, a professor might be handed her course evaluation results or a telephone solicitor could be given information on how many of his contacts actually purchased a particular product. Such knowledge of results should help the professor and solicitor improve job performance in the future. Informational feedback is *non*evaluative—in other words, it should be transmitted to the employee without judgments as to how good or bad the performance was.

---

[15]O. Mayr, "The Origins of Feedback Control," *Scientific American,* 1970, no. 223, p. 111.

2   Corrective Feedback   A manager can be evaluative (judgmental) in providing an employee with knowledge of results. The purpose of corrective feedback, however, is not to criticize and punish but, rather, to inform and correct. The famous basketball coach John Wooden, of the University of California, Los Angeles, was a master at using corrective feedback effectively:

> Observation of Wooden's behavior in practice sessions showed that while 50% of his contacts with his players amounted to straightforward instructions, no less than 75% of his contacts were instructive in nature. He used instructions to simultaneously point out a mistake and indicate the correct way of performing. Wooden's corrective feedback centered around the task at hand, not around the personality of the player. . . . An effective manager, like an effective coach, must not only point out mistakes but also get the individual headed in the right direction with appropriate instructions.[16]

3   Reinforcing Feedback   When an employee is successful (productive) in the workplace, reinforcing feedback is used to reward the job performance. The praise given to employees at Emery Air Freight Corporation (see p. 66) is an example of reinforcing feedback (simply telling them how they did would be an example of informational feedback). Which kind of reinforcing feedback you give your workers will depend on their particular needs. As Kreitner correctly observes:

> Managers can . . . diagnose the specific reinforcing consequences to which subordinates currently respond. Careful observation of job performance soon reveals whether or not an individual responds to praise, money, additional responsibility, job rotation, status symbols, formal recognition, peer approval, or any other of the many consequences of job behavior. In a manner of speaking, managers must "fine-tune" reinforcing feedback to suit the individual. No quick and easy panaceas exist in this area.[17]

Providing Feedback

There are many opportunities for you to provide employees with feedback on the job. It can be done during formalized time periods set

---

[16]R. Kreitner, "People Are Systems, Too: Filling the Feedback Vacuum," *Business Horizons,* November 1977, pp. 56–57.

[17]Ibid., p. 57.

aside for it (for instance, during performance appraisals) or spontaneously during the workday in response to particular employee behavior. To be most effective, feedback should be *specific* and *clearly understandable* to the worker. Feedback won't help if your employees can't identify it with the behavior you're talking about; likewise, telling subordinates how they have performed in statistical terms won't make a difference if they don't understand statistics in the first place.

Don't forget that feedback is essential to learning—and it can be rewarding, too. When you manage, why not make it a part of your worthplace; if you do, you'll increase the chances that your business charts will be looking up.

REWARD 10: SOCIAL PARTICIPATION

Do you recall Mr. Monotone, the professor who liked to scratch his head? We got him to increase his little habit by giving him social approval—a reward that satisfied his social needs.

Many workers—managers as well as their subordinates—respond with greater productivity and satisfaction when their social needs are fulfilled in the workplace. This is because many of us are concerned with *affiliation:* being around other people and being accepted by them. People with social needs want to "belong"; they desire social relationships and the chance to interact with others—desires that can be satisfied in the worthplace if a manager provides the proper environment for social participation to take place.

Basically, there are two types of social participation that can be rewarding for a worker on the job: interaction with peers and interaction with the manager.

Types of Social Participation

1   Interaction with Peers   We have already seen (in our discussion of job enrichment) how autonomous work teams are created to help fend off boredom and make the working experience more rewarding. In your own managerial situation there will normally be ample opportunity to encourage the development of compatible work groups as a means of satisfying social needs through social participation. One way to do this is participative management (see Reward 7), having subordinates meet as a group with the supervisor to discuss various issues that affect them. Another way is the development of "company spirit" (see Reward 11), encouraging social participation through various social events and team-building efforts. For an example of how one company has encouraged social participation with gratifying results, see Box 7-5.

2   Interaction with the Manager   This is an area many supervisors overlook, sometimes with serious consequences. It is important to realize that in many cases the social relationships you establish with your subordinates can have a definite impact on their productivity level and job satisfaction. Managers who are also *leaders* develop effective interpersonal relationships with employees—they are able to

---

BOX 7-5

IF THE SHOE FITS, WEAR IT*

The R. G. Barry Corporation manufactures footwear out of Columbus, Ohio. In 1969 the company decided to use social participation (in the form of "teamwork") as a way to increase worker productivity and satisfaction on the job. This required conversion of an individual, every-worker-for-himself incentive system to a team process. Three hundred production workers were organized into teams ranging from eight to twelve employees. Each team was then responsible for product manufacture from cut stock to finished product. Teams were also allowed to participate in the company's decision-making activities (see Reward 7), an opportunity that was well received by the workers.

After a rocky start, the team approach took hold. The results? "Absenteeism and personnel turnover declined by 50 percent; products sent back for reworking have been cut by two-thirds; downtime diminished significantly; training costs are down 50 percent; and total output is up 35 percent. Wages also increased 35 percent from 1969 to 1973."

One machine operator summed up employee feelings toward the new social participation in these words: "Before, everyone was on his own and no one cared about helping their fellow employee. Now everyone is dependent upon everybody else. I know in my case I think twice before taking a day off because I know if I do it will affect my team."

*The material in Box 7-5 was based on the following article: B. Shelton, " 'Team Spirit' Results in Higher Productivity, Job Satisfaction," *Commerce Today*, Sept. 30, 1974, pp. 5–6.

---

transmit a sense of caring and interpersonal enthusiasm which workers appreciate (see pp. 132–135).

Of course, there are times when interpersonal interaction won't be a vital factor in the workplace. First of all, not all workers have social needs, and if they don't, then the reward value of social participation will be diminished. Secondly, not all jobs allow for social participation. How, for example, can a manager who oversees a group of salespeople working separate territories encourage social participation on the job? Finally, on some jobs the employees might prefer to work alone or, when placed together, become too competitive or hostile with each other.

As with all the rewards in this chapter, you as manager will have to test social participation to see if it's effective in your particular work environment. Does social participation make your subordinates more productive and satisfied? If it does, then fine—it can be used with good results. If it doesn't, well—there are thirteen other rewards waiting to be used. Chances are excellent that some of them will help you get the results you're looking for.

REWARD 11: COMPANY SPIRIT

In central Florida there is a company that makes small aircraft, the kind that hold four to six passengers. It is not a large-scale operation—but it is a spirited one. Each time a plane rolls off the assembly line, the employees are given time off to gather around the finished aircraft and have a celebration (sometimes a picnic), a kind of "product send-off party" when the new owner comes to take delivery of his plane.

Across the country, California-based Kaiser Aluminum & Chemical Corporation gives its employees "inspirational" gifts—everything from frisbees to T-shirts—in an attempt to "motivate the work force" and "make people aware that their small unit is part of a large company."[18]

What do the aircraft company and Kaiser Aluminum have in common? Both organizations are directly fostering esprit de corps among company employees—attempting to increase worker production and satisfaction through the development of company spirit.

[18]Kaiser's efforts are described in D. Clutterbuck's article "Motivation Programme Is a Give-Away," *International Management,* August 1977, pp. 40–41.

BOX 7-6

COMPANY SPIRIT—IBM STYLE*

What image comes to mind when you hear the initials IBM? A huge computer? A massive building housing thousands of employees? Most people think of IBM as a big, impersonal corporation relentlessly spreading technology around the globe. These individuals would no doubt be surprised to learn that International Business Machines Corporation is called "Mother IBM" by many of those who work for it—recognition of the fact that IBM very actively and successfully develops company spirit among its employees.

In a *Newsweek* article, Allan Mayer and Michael Ruby describe some of the ways IBM establishes *esprit de corps* among its employees:

> More than any other major corporation in America, IBM smothers its employees with a dazzling array of womb-to-tomb benefits, ingenious motivational perks and sophisticated self-improvement programs. Not only does IBM pay its 300,000 employees generous salaries and cover their medical bills, it also counsels, trains and entertains them, supports their favorite charities and helps with their children's education. And uniquely among American corporations, it virtually guarantees its workers lifetime job security.

What is the result of all this "mothering"? A great many loyal, productive and satisfied employees. And some happy spouses, too. The wife of one IBM employee expressed her feelings this way: "IBM embodies all the values we hold sacred—worth of the individual, pursuit of excellence, brotherhood, the work ethic. . . . And over the years, the children absorb this. I do feel that the company takes a personal interest in me and my children, that it provides us with security and cares about us."

Want a good example of company spirit? Read the wife's comments again, and you'll reach the bottom line.

*The material in Box 7-6 is based on A. Mayer and M. Ruby, "One Firm's Family," *Newsweek*, Nov. 21, 1977, p. 82ff.

Exactly what is company spirit? Company spirit is a sense of pride, dedication, and loyalty to the organization one works for. It's kind of like patriotism, but in this case employees feel a sense of commitment to their employer. When workers feel this way about the company they work for—when they have company spirit—chances are they will be highly productive and satisfied on the job (see Box 7-6).

By now you are probably asking "How can I, as a manager, create a sense of esprit de corps among my employees?" You might want to try one or more of the suggestions below. Each has been used successfully in the business community. Whether any or all of these approaches work for you will depend, to a great degree, on the size of your work force, the needs of your particular employees, your budget, and the willingness of your organization to actively support "company spirit" programs in the workplace.

1 Develop work teams throughout the company or among the employees you supervise (see Reward 10 and Box 7-5).

2 Involve employees in the decision-making activities of the company (see Reward 7).

3 Sponsor various social functions for company employees (for example, picnics and outings).

4 Sponsor company sports teams.

5 Undertake activities that will make your employees proud to be associated with the company. For example, some businesses sponsor little league teams or civic activities; others conduct advertising campaigns that emphasize the "good deeds" they are doing in the community.

6 Conduct friendly competitions between various work teams in the company (for example, give an award to the team with highest output or best safety record). Be careful, however, to make sure the competition doesn't get out of hand.

7 Help your employees identify with the products they produce. Some businesses, like the aircraft company in the earlier example, do this by inviting all employees to see the product once it's completed. Other organizations encourage employee identification by having them sign the product they produce or in a like manner have them take personal responsibility for what they have created.

In many ways, a caring organization—one that practices the human use of human resources—will almost automatically increase its chances of developing company spirit. A caring company is like a caring manager—it brings out the best in workers, including higher productivity and job satisfaction.

REWARD 12: THE OPPORTUNITY TO ACHIEVE
AND ADVANCE IN THE ORGANIZATION

When employees reach the upper rungs of the Maslow hierarchy, they become responsive to rewards that satisfy their esteem and self-actualization needs. The opportunity to achieve is important to these individuals; so is the opportunity to advance—to be promoted, to rise in the organization.

Time and time again I have watched businesses lose their most capable employees because they failed to provide them with jobs where accomplishment and advancement were possible. Don't make such a mistake. Keep apprised of your employees' progress and check with them frequently to see how they feel about their development within the company.

Do your best to see that all employees have job assignments where achievement and advancement are possible. Many times this will require changing your workers' assignments and responsibilities to keep pace with their growth and development in the workplace (see the discussion of job enrichment under Reward 6). This will require some effort, but it will be effort well invested—particularly when you consider that the people who want to achieve and advance in the organization are normally the most motivated and capable employees you'll be supervising. You don't want to lose them, and making it possible for them to achieve and advance in the organization is one good way to keep them productive, satisfied—and around.

REWARD 13: DEGREES OF FREEDOM AT WORK

I recently spoke with a department store buyer who was angry because she might have to punch in and out of work on a time clock. "I didn't have to do that under the old manager," she argued.

"What about the other people in your office," I inquired, "don't they have to punch in and out?"

"They're hourly workers," the buyer scoffed, "I'm a professional, I don't work by the clock."

Although this particular employee sounds a bit egotistical and spoiled, her concern does reflect a problem common to many workers as they climb the organizational ladder and the Maslow hierarchy: the need for more degrees of freedom on the job.

When I speak of degrees of freedom in work, I am referring to the level of personal autonomy and responsibility a person has on the job. Employees with high degrees of freedom in the workplace are pretty much their own boss when it comes to organizing their work and making decisions. Employees with low degrees of freedom have very little say in what they do or how they do it—they are, as some managers are fond of saying, "closely watched."

Now it is true that some types of jobs require closer supervision than others. It is also true that certain workers prefer to be closely supervised and shun the opportunity for more personal autonomy in the workplace. In these cases, giving workers degrees of freedom can cause difficulties. But what about those jobs that can be effectively performed by employees working under their own "recognizance"? And what about those workers who covet more degrees of freedom in the workplace? In these circumstances managers would be well-advised to loosen the reins of control and let employees have more say in the conduct of their work.

To determine what level of freedom you should give your workers, ask (and answer) these two questions:

1   Are my employees doing the kind of work that requires constant managerial supervision, or can I step back and let them have more control over their job activities?
2   Do my employees want more degrees of freedom on the job?

As far as the second question is concerned, you won't go very far afield if you follow this guideline. Generally, employees with higher level needs will be most rewarded by greater degrees of freedom on the job. If you turn back to Figure 5-2 you will note three things self-actualizing people want out of a job: (1) creative and challenging work; (2) responsibility for decision making; and (3) flexibility and freedom. These three wants can be satisfied by giving your employees greater degrees of freedom in the workplace. And if they're capable workers, giving them greater freedom will make your job easier in the bargain!

REWARD 14: PLEASANT FORMS
OF MODERATE DISTRACTION

In 1965 a team of behavioral scientists conducted an interesting study with some Yale University undergraduates. One group of students read a series of four persuasive messages in a room well stocked with soft drinks and peanuts. The students were encouraged to sample the refreshments as they read—which they all did. A second group of students was presented with the same four messages to read, but in a room where no refreshments were available. Both groups of students were asked, before and after reading the four messages, certain key questions, which enabled the investigators to assess their degree of opinion change (if any) in response to the persuasive appeals. In other words, the scientists were able to ascertain if any of the students had been swayed by the four persuasive appeals.

What were the results of the study? The students who ate while they read were more persuaded by each of the four messages than were those students who read the same messages without food.[19]

On the basis of this study and several others,[20] behavioral scientists now believe that, in general, *persuasive appeals become more powerful when presented in conjunction with moderately distracting stimuli (for example, food) which positively reward the individual.*

How can this information be of use to you as a manager on the job? It suggests that if you want to be more persuasive with your employees (have them do what you want them to do), it might help if you utilize some pleasant forms of moderate distraction while making your requests. Even more important, pleasant forms of moderate distraction can increase worker satisfaction, not only because they are rewards in themselves, but also because they act as a boredom reducer in the workplace (see *Job Enrichment* under Reward 6).

There are several kinds of pleasant distraction you can use in the workplace (such as music and workspace alterations), but the most practical, versatile, and effective one for our purposes is . . . *food.*

[19]I. Janis, D. Kaye, and P. Kirschner, "Facilitating Effects of 'Eating-While-Reading' on Responsiveness to Persuasive Communications," *Journal of Personality and Social Psychology,* vol. 1, 1965, pp. 181–186.

[20]See M. Karlins and H. Abelson, *Persuasion: How Opinions and Attitudes Are Changed,* Springer, New York, 1970.

BOX 7-7

SOME FOOD FOR THOUGHT

For many years Fran Tarkenton was a superstar in the National Football League. As a quarterback for the Minnesota Vikings, he led his team all the way to the Superbowl on several occasions. Many people wonder how he did it. Some say it was his scrambling ability under pressure. Others speak of his pinpoint passing. Would you believe me if I told you it was because he used pleasant forms of moderate distraction? Probably not. But all-star, veteran quarterback Fran Tarkenton was known to give out candy to his teammates after they made a good play.* Now there's a man who understands the relationship between productivity and satisfaction on the job!

*Reported in L. Moore's article, "Motivation through Positive Reinforcement," *Supervisory Management,* October 1976, p. 8.

Salespeople have long recognized and utilized the power of food. The selling power of the client lunch is widely accepted in business circles. When it comes time to sign the contract—to close the deal—it is often accomplished over dessert. "A well-fed customer is a purchasing customer," as one salesperson expressed it.

Does this mean you'll have to take your subordinates to dinner every time you want to use pleasant forms of moderate distraction? Definitely not. The bent-elbow-and-heaping-forkful approach might be suitable for special occasions, but it is certainly inappropriate as an everyday kind of reward at work. It is appropriate, however, to serve coffee and doughnuts at staff meetings—particularly if the meetings are early in the morning. Even if you have to pay for these "goodies" out of pocket, I think you will find the benefits far outweigh the costs. It is amazing how a few doughnuts and cups of coffee can perk people up and put them in a cooperative, productive frame of mind. I know managers who also have coffee and small bowls of snacks in their offices, to offer to subordinates when they come in to discuss items of business. According to the managers, this helps open channels of communication and creates good feelings.

Like all the rewards we have discussed in this chapter, pleasant forms of moderate distraction will work better in some job settings than others. How effective will the reward be with your employees? The best way to find out is give pleasant distractions a try in your workplace.

Some Recommendations

1   Use Moderate, Not Intense, Distractions   If a distraction is too strong, it can cause a decrease (rather than an increase) in productivity. For example, some companies pipe music over their intercoms. If this music is too distracting, employees end up concentrating on the tunes rather than on their work.

2   Use Pleasant, Not Unpleasant, Distractions   Research studies clearly show that unpleasant distractions (even moderate forms of unpleasant distractions) reduce worker satisfaction and productivity—exactly the opposite of what you want. In this context, be sure you *know* what your individual employees consider pleasant or unpleasant distractions. For example, some employees might find hard rock music a pleasant form of moderate distraction, while others might consider it an unpleasant form of intense distraction. Play it safe: observe your workers' reactions to the distractions you use. That way you'll know what they think about them.

WORK AS ITS OWN REWARD

In this chapter I have described fourteen rewards you can use to make your employees more productive and satisfied in the workplace.

"But," you ask, "what if my employees are already satisfied with their work?" In that case, count yourself among the fortunate. As management expert Lewis Moore indicates: "The more rewarding the work is perceived to be by the worker, the less need for supervision—except to specify results wanted."[21]

Unfortunately, not that many workers are naturally turned on by their jobs, and "in order to get the same level of motivation from employees who perceive less reward in their work, the difference in reinforcement must come from management. . . ."[22]

[21]L. Moore, "Motivation through Positive Reinforcement," *Supervisory Management,* October 1976, p. 9.
[22]Ibid.

This is where you come in. If your workers are not already satisfied with their jobs, you can help them by utilizing the fourteen rewards to create an environment that fulfills their needs and turns the workplace into a worthplace. In other words, your goal is to use rewards to create a worthplace more satisfying and meaningful to each individual employee.

Work does not have to be a four-letter word. Through such techniques as job enrichment, social participation, and employee involvement in decision making, you can encourage employees to get "into" what they are doing—help build a job to a point where it will become intrinsically interesting and motivationally self-sustaining.

Of course, you won't always be successful in getting an employee to the point where work becomes its own reward; but even then you can use rewards like praise, public recognition, and leisure time to make the job more palatable. Either way, you accomplish your ultimate goal: making the workplace a worthplace, where employees can satisfy their needs and be more productive at the same time.

Chapter 8

How to Administer Workplace Rewards Most Effectively

Knowing the rewards you can use on the job is important, but you must also learn the rules for using those rewards most effectively.

Aerospace industry manager

Before I present the rules for administering workplace rewards most effectively, let me briefly restate the major points discussed earlier.

A BRIEF REVIEW

From our discussion of behavior modification and Maslow's need hierarchy you now know that (1) individual workers have individual needs and will behave in ways that lead to the satisfaction of those needs and that (2) behavior which is rewarded will be maintained or even increase in frequency. Putting this information together, your goal as a manager is to reinforce appropriate work behavior with rewards that satisfy the particular needs of individual employees. This should enhance worker productivity and satisfy worker needs, thus establishing the + + relationship essential to making the workplace a worthplace.

Accomplishing this goal will require you to complete successfully a three-step process:

Step 1   You will have to identify the specific needs of your individual workers.

Step 2   You will have to satisfy each worker's specific need(s) with the appropriate reward(s).

Step 3   You will have to administer worker rewards effectively.

Step 1 is discussed in Chapter 5 and at the end of Chapter 6. Step 2 is discussed in Chapter 7, where you will find the fourteen rewards you can use in motivating your workers. Step 3 is discussed below. Here you will find the basic guidelines for administering rewards in a manner that maximizes worker productivity and satisfaction on the job.

SOME MAJOR GUIDELINES FOR ADMINISTERING REWARDS EFFECTIVELY

Guideline 1   Know what kind of performance you want from your employees and let them know what your expectations are.

To administer rewards effectively, both you and your employees should have a common understanding of what is considered effective behavior (good output) on the job. This means you should first determine in your own mind the kinds of employee action that will lead to good job performance, and then you should explain to your subordinates what steps they can take to achieve that good performance and receive rewards.

If you don't take the time to tell your employees what your performance goals are and how they can be reached, then your subordinates will have to find out for themselves, usually through trial-and-error behavior on the job—and that is a tremendous waste of time, effort, and productivity. It doesn't do much for creating job satisfaction either.

Here are three questions I'd like you to ask yourself as a manager:

1 Have I determined what constitutes good performance in the workplace?

2 Have I communicated to my employees (a) my definition and standard of good performance; (b) the kinds of job behavior they should undertake to achieve good job performance; and (c) what they must do to receive the various rewards?

3 Do I have a method of accurately and fairly assessing the level of worker performance on the job?

If you can answer yes to all three questions, then you're in good shape as far as Guideline 1 is concerned.

Guideline 2 Give your subordinates those rewards that best satisfy their particular needs.

Put another way, the reward that works best is the reward that satisfies a worker's need(s) most successfully (see Box 8-1). Your goal should be the achievement of a match between workers' needs and the rewards they receive on the job. To do this effectively, you should know about the kinds of needs employees have and the rewards associated with them (see Chapters 5–7).

BOX 8-1

THE SOLID PINK CADILLAC

Mary Kay Ash retired as training director for World Gift, a decorative accessories company, in 1963. Not satisfied with the "life of leisure," she decided to start her own company, which in 14 years has turned into a $50 million cosmetics business.

How did she do it? One way was by giving her employees rewards that best satisfied their particular needs. For the women who sold her beauty products, such rewards ran the gambit from pocket calculators to pink cadillacs.

Recognizing that many women "haven't had a round of applause since they graduated from school," Ms. Ash made sure there were plenty of plaudits for her personnel. "On Awards Night," she explains, "we get 8,000 people, all of whom come to Dallas at their own expense. Thousands of prizes are awarded, ranging from the keys to a Cadillac to diamond bumblebee pins. We crown the queens of sales and recruitment and present them with prizes and flowers and scepters, accompanied by standing ovations and musical fanfares."*

Mary Kay Ash understood her employees' needs and the kinds of rewards that would satisfy those needs. And that's good business—from everyone's point of view.

*Quote taken from an interview with Mary Kay Ash, "Flying High on an Idea," *Nation's Business*, August 1978, pp. 41ff.

Some managers try to guess what needs their workers have and what rewards they'd like to receive. As we saw on page 51, this can lead to some very inaccurate estimates. If you want to obtain greatest accuracy in identifying which rewards work best with which employees, observe your subordinates as you give them reinforcement. That way you can pinpoint the rewards that work best with each employee. Such information is particularly valuable, because in most instances you'll have to pick from a number of different rewards to use at any given need level of the Maslow hierarchy.

Also, continue to observe your subordinates even *after* you have ascertained their needs and the rewards they value most. This is crucial because workers' needs can change over time, and so can their attitudes toward particular rewards. For example, some workers get bored with certain rewards if they're used too often, causing them to lose their effectiveness. If you continue to observe your subordinates, you will be alerted to these changes and be able to take corrective action. Otherwise, you might miss such changes entirely and wonder why you suddenly wind up with a disgruntled, unproductive employee.

Remember, the best way to see if a reward "works" is to administer it to an employee and watch the results. If the rewarded behavior is maintained or increases in frequency, chances are the reward is effective.

In observing Guideline 2, it will help to keep the following points in mind (in addition to those already mentioned):

1 Many employees have several different needs at the same time, thus allowing you to use several different kinds of rewards in such circumstances.

2 Certain rewards (such as money) can satisfy more than one human need, and certain needs can be satisfied by more than one reward. Choose the reward that works best for the individual worker in question.

3 Be on the lookout for boredom effects if you use the same reward frequently with a particular employee. Try not to overuse a reinforcement so that it loses its effectiveness. Using more than one kind of reward, or decreasing use of the same reward, will reduce the risk of "reward boredom."

4 Try to familiarize yourself with all fourteen rewards and how they can be used to best advantage. The more rewards you can utilize comfortably and effectively, the better manager you'll be.

Guideline 3 You don't have to reward a desired behavior everytime it occurs.

Many managers believe that the best way to keep employee performance high is to reinforce effective behavior everytime it occurs. In reality, quite the opposite can occur: rewarding specific actions everytime they occur can actually decrease performance levels in the long run.

Initially, when an employee is learning a new task, it helps to reward the employee frequently, so that the behavior becomes fixed in the person's response pattern. Once the behavior has become established, however, it is appropriate to *gradually* cut back the frequency of rewards and move toward *intermittent* ("variable") reinforcement of effective performance. By rewarding behavior intermittently (rather than everytime it occurs) you gain three benefits:

1 You don't need as much of the reward (for instance, if you're using money as a reinforcement, it will last longer if administered intermittently rather than continuously).

2 The chance that the worker becomes bored with the reward through overuse will be reduced.

3 Intermittent reinforcement sustains higher levels of performance over longer periods of time. Employees keep working with the
expectation that their reward is "right around the corner." This type of
thinking keeps gamblers frantically pumping coins into slot machines.
On one-armed bandits, "reinforcement in the form of winning is not
dispensed each time nor on a regular basis, but on a random or
intermittent basis. Therefore, the player is highly motivated to
continue playing; the next play may be a winner."[1]

Now comes an interesting question. How intermittent should
your intermittent reinforcement be? In other words, how often should
you reward your employees for work well done? The answer is, often
enough to sustain quality job performance. When you use reinforcement, observe the impact of your rewards on your employees'
behavior. If worker performance level remains high, chances are that
your frequency of reinforcement is "on target." If performance drops,
however, you might want to decrease or increase the amount of
reinforcement until you reach a level that brings employee performance up to optimum levels. In doing so, the following points might
help:

1 Too much as well as too little reinforcement can lead to a
decline in job performance. Do not reinforce so frequently that the
reward loses potency or so infrequently as to "extinguish" appropriate
behaviors.
2 Different employees require different amounts of reinforcement to keep their performance levels high. By observing your
workers, you will be able to determine the ideal intermittent schedule
for any particular employee.

Guideline 4 Reward desired behaviors immediately after they
occur.

The sooner you can reward an employee for superior job performance, the more effective that reinforcement will be. Conversely, the
longer the delay between the desired behavior and the ensuing
reward, the less effective the reinforcement becomes. This timing-of-
reinforcement effect is clearly documented in the behavioral science

[1]R. Beatty and C. Schneier, "A Case for Positive Reinforcement," *Business
Horizons,* April 1975, p. 61.

literature and says, in effect, that you must act quickly once you become aware of reinforceable behavior.

Of course, sometimes it is not possible for a manager to reinforce an employee immediately for desired work behavior. For example, two weeks may pass before a manager learns that a salesperson has closed a big deal; or a manager may be away from the office when an employee does something outstanding. What then? Fortunately, reinforcement is still possible, but under these circumstances it is vitally important that the manager clearly state what the reward is for. It is not enough to say, "This bonus is for good work on the job." The work behavior in question must be specifically identified by saying, for example, "This bonus is to recognize your achievement in closing the Johnson account." It is necessary that the worker establish a bond between a specific reward and a specific behavior—otherwise behavior modification won't work. And it's up to you as manager to reinforce in a manner that makes such bonding possible.

Guideline 5   Whenever possible use reward rather than punishment in the workplace.

Perhaps you've wondered why I spent a whole chapter discussing workplace rewards and not a single page examining punishments. It is because I believe that rewards are more effective in establishing desired behaviors and avoiding undesirable ones. Professor Thomas Rotondi has this to say:

> . . . punishment tends to suppress rather than eliminate undesirable behavior. When the punishment ends, the undesirable behavior may be repeated. What's more, applying punishment to individuals may also create such undesirable side effects as fears, anxieties, erratic behavior, vindictiveness, or subtle sabotage.[2]

Much of my thinking about reward versus punishment is reflected in the fable of the old man and his coat. It seems the old gent was spotted by the spirits of Winter and Summer as he walked along a path in an enchanted forest. The two spirits were in a competitive mood that afternoon, and suddenly the spirit of Winter said, "I'll bet you I

[2]T. Rotondi, "Behavior Modification on the Job," *Supervisory Management*, February 1976, p. 26.

can strip that man of the coat he's wearing faster than you can." "It's a bet," the spirit of Summer replied, "you can go first."

The spirit of Winter took a deep breath and blew up a raging arctic storm that whipped through the forest and buffeted the old man about like a leaf. He gathered his tattered coat around him and hung on for dear life. The wind threatened to tear the coat right off his body. Every button was ripped away, and still the old man hung on gamely. Finally, the spirit of Winter tired and the storm dissipated. The old man brushed the debris off what was left of his coat and took a few tentative steps.

"It's my turn now," said the spirit of Summer, and with a nod sent the clouds scurrying across the sky and turned the sun's full radiance on the forest. The old man turned his face to the sun and felt the welcome, penetrating heat. It felt good. He took off his coat and continued on his way.

The moral? It is better if an employee wants to do something than if he has to do it. This is the spirit and essence of the human use of human resources; the cornerstone of the ++ relationship in the worthplace.

Does this mean I'm against all punishment in the workplace? No. There will be times when, having exhausted all avenues of positive reinforcement, your only recourse will be punitive action. Yet, even then, punishment can be administered in a constructive fashion—not for revenge but to get the worker back "on track." And, of course, punishment should always be done in private, as your goal is to educate, not humiliate, an employee.

Administered in the proper spirit—as a form of constructive criticism—even punishment can play a meaningful role in the worthplace. Before you opt for using it, however, it might be instructive to consider the words of management authority Bernard Rosenbaum: "When it comes to supervising people, rarely is there too much positive reinforcement. Managers who encounter undesirable behavior should ask themselves when and in what way the desired behavior was last reinforced."[3]

Guideline 6 Give rewards only when they are deserved.

[3]B. Rosenbaum, "Understanding and Using Motivation," *Supervisory Management,* January 1979, p. 12.

In other words, reinforcement should be sincere and earned. If an employee doesn't deserve praise, then don't give it; it is better to withhold a compliment than give one dishonestly. Not only is such behavior unethical, it is bad management. Employees are quick to detect your motives; they see such reinforcement as cheap manipulation—which it is. Don't behave in such a manner; it is not humane and it doesn't work.

Chapter 9

A Personal View of Effective Leadership

The lack of leadership in industry and government is the chief difficulty in this country.

William McCleery

I love to browse through bookstores. On a recent visit I noticed that an entire shelf was set aside for books on sexual techniques. Above the shelf someone had written a note claiming, "These techniques can make *you* a better lover." While I was mulling over that bit of advertising, a student walked up and showed me an armload of business books she had just purchased. "I want to make it big in my job," she explained, "and these books have the techniques I'll need to know to become an effective leader."

Do you find all this lamentable? I do. It is a sad commentary on the human condition that people believe effective loving or leading can be reduced to a series of techniques.

Please don't misunderstand me. I'm not saying that techniques are unimportant—they just aren't the whole story or, for that matter, the most important part of it. Take leadership, for example. There are literally dozens of techniques you can use to become a more effective supervisor, but those techniques by themselves won't make you a true leader. There is an ingredient missing, something else that has to be there. It's like trying to bake bread without yeast. You can still do it, but you'll never get the dough to rise past a certain point. As a manager you can use the various techniques to sharpen your supervisory skills, but you'll never *rise* to great leadership without adding the missing ingredient—the ingredient I call the "human component" of leadership.

What, exactly, is this human component so crucial for effective leadership? It is actually three things: *love, enthusiasm, and dedication.* It is no wonder that the first letters of these four words add up to another word:

L OVE + E NTHUSIASM + A ND + D EDICATION = L.E.A.D.

The manager who knows how to L.E.A.D. becomes a L.E.A.D.E.R., because L OVE, E NTHUSIASM, A ND D EDICATION E ARN R ESPECT—and that is basic to a meaningful bond between manager and employee.

Love, Enthusiasm, and Dedication Defined

These words have special meanings when utilized in the workplace, so it is best that we define them now.

Love   Another word for this term is "caring." What I am referring to here is the capacity of managers to love (in a caring sense) their employees, to sincerely care for them as human beings. This sense of caring is something which can be learned but can't be faked. Workers are quick to sense whether their managers truly care for them. If employees feel this caring is present, it can contribute mightily to their productivity and satisfaction in the workplace. If, on the other hand, they feel a manager lacks this capacity, then no amount of techniques—however well executed—will ever make that manager a great leader.

Let me illustrate the importance of love/caring with an example from where I work. In my department I have a colleague who is an outstanding scholar and a dedicated academician. I took it for granted he was also a topnotch teacher: after all, he knows his subject matter better than anyone else at the university, and I have seen him spend many hours preparing his lectures. You can imagine my surprise, then, when several students stopped by my office to complain about my colleague's poor teaching performance.

"What's wrong with him," I wanted to know, "Is he a boring speaker?"

"No," they responded.

"Is he unprepared for class?"

"No," again.

"Are his tests unfair?"

"No," again.

"Does he miss classes?"

"No," a fourth time.

"Well, what *is* it then?"

Silence. Finally a student came up with this response: "I guess it's not really his teaching that's the problem . . . it's a feeling I get that he doesn't really *care* about me as a person, that I'm somebody to be tolerated as part of the job."

"That's right," another student broke in. "The man is aloof and distant . . . he doesn't treat his students like human beings."

Love. It's a vital part of effective leadership.

Enthusiasm   Enthusiastic managers are persons who put energy into their work, who bring a sense of spirit and excitement to the workplace. Enthusiasm is contagious. If managers have it, chances are better that their workers will have it, too. Lethargy, unfortunately, is also contagious. When managers walk into the office looking disinterested and bored, is it any wonder their employees become listless and unmotivated as well? As a manager you set a mood tone for your employees, and it is important that the mood be a positive one. But, in being enthusiastic, two points are worth remembering:

1   To be enthusiastic you don't have to be "rah rah" or "gung ho." A quiet enthusiasm is just as potent as animated enthusiasm—just so long as employees can sense your positive, interested attitude toward work.

2   As a manager you don't have to be enthusiastic about your work every moment of every working day. Nobody expects you to like your job all the time! There will be days when you come to work in a sour mood; there will also be times when your work gets you down. In these circumstances, it is perfectly all right to act "down in the dumps." Employees don't expect you to feign enthusiasm when you feel like hell. In fact, if you are usually enthusiastic in the workplace, a few "off" days will tend to reinforce that general enthusiasm.

Enthusiasm. It's an important part of the charisma generated by effective leaders.

Dedication   Another word for dedication can be "commitment." Dedicated managers are committed to their work, and they pass along this sense of dedication to their employees.

Many managers ask me how they can be sure they're dedicated to their work. This is not a silly question, as being immersed in a job day after day sometimes limits our ability to judge work effectively. There are two ways you can take a reading of your job dedication level.

1   *Monitor your enthusiasm:* Keep tabs on your level of job enthusiasm over time. Dedication and enthusiasm are intimately linked: people who are dedicated to their jobs are almost always enthusiastic about them. Thus if you sense your enthusiasm for work is waning, it might be a sign of eroding dedication as well.

2   *Ask yourself two questions upon awakening in the morning:* (1) Am I looking forward to today? (2) Would I rather be doing something else than the work I'm in? If you find yourself *consistently* answering no to the first question and yes to the second question, it is doubtful you are generating much dedication to your job. And if that's the way *you* feel about your work, how can you expect your employees to feel any differently about theirs.

Dedication. It's a vital source of strength for effective leaders.

A Personal Request

Leadership is more than a series of techniques to be mastered. It is first and foremost a human being *being human*. It is a manager who understands the human component in the leadership equation—who cares about employees and is enthusiastic about and dedicated to the job. It is a manager who uses behavioral science techniques to establish a ++ relationship on the job, a *worthplace* where employees can satisfy their needs and be productive at the same time.

Of course, by my definition, there are not many managers who qualify as leaders in the contemporary business world. For that matter there are not many leaders among parents, teachers, and politicians either. That is because most of us have not learned to L.E.A.D. in a humane way.

Which brings me to my request: Just because there are so many inhumane managers in the work world doesn't mean you have to further populate their ranks. *If you feel you cannot or will not inject the human component into your leadership behavior, don't become a manager in the first place—at least not the kind of manager who has to consistently interact with subordinates.* It just won't be fair to you, and it certainly won't be fair to your employees. If your subordinate wants to be uncaring, unenthusiastic, and undedicated on the job, that is bad enough; but if you as a manager feel that way, then you are setting an example that can affect many other lives (as well as your own) in a negative way.

Some of you might not agree with, or honor, this request. That is your choice. As the chapter title suggests, this is my personal view of leadership, and you might not share it. But I do believe it is a correct view, and I, for one, certainly wouldn't want to work under a manager who disagreed with it. Think about it, would you?

Section Three

How to Succeed in Business without Really Dying

Chapter 10

How to Keep Physically and Mentally Alert on the Job

You can't help others if you can't help yourself.

Transportation industry manager

Our family physician is a busy man. I stopped by his office one morning for a routine physical exam and marveled at the sheer number of patients being shuffled in and out of doors as the doctor moved briskly from one examination room to the next.

When it came time for my appointment, I didn't wait for the physician to speak as he barreled through the door. "How are you feeling today, Doctor," I asked, smiling a hello.

The question stopped him in his tracks. He groped for words and then just gave up, his mouth half open.

"What's the matter?" I inquired.

"It's just . . . that . . . well, nobody ever asked me how *I* felt before."

As a manager you're going to be in basically the same predicament as my family physician. Your employees are going to expect you to listen to their everyday gripes and problems, without considering that you, too, have your hassles and difficulties.

This is unfortunate because you're a human being with human needs just like your subordinates. And it is important that you recognize and deal with these needs, even if your employees don't. It would be bitter irony indeed if, as an expert in human resource management, you couldn't manage the most important human resource of all—yourself.

Up to this point we have concentrated on what you can do to help others meet their needs and be more productive in the workplace; this final chapter focuses on what you can do to increase *your* satisfaction and productivity on the job. My concern here will be with showing you how to succeed in business without really dying—how you can be healthy, happy, *and* successful in the workplace.

A PINK SLIP NOBODY WANTS

Here's a brainteaser for you. Steve Johnson is a dynamic, aggressive executive with a Fortune 500 company. For the past 15 years he's risen steadily through the corporate ranks, gaining respect and recognition in the business community. Yet, a few months short of his forty-fifth birthday, Steve Johnson suddenly loses his job. Why?

Because Steve Johnson dropped dead—irrevocably cut down at the height of a promising career. Unusual? Unfortunately not. It has been estimated that loss of production due to premature deaths costs American business in excess of $20 billion yearly—and that figure doesn't even start to approach the billions more lost through health-related absenteeism.

Yet the real tragedy of Steve Johnson goes beyond economic profit and loss—even beyond the personal loss of those who loved him. *The real tragedy of Steve Johnson is that he died unnecessarily.* When a young man like Steve Johnson succumbs to a stroke or coronary seizure, we are grimly reminded of our own mortality; yet in most cases it didn't have to happen (at least at such a young age). It was preventable. By making certain medically recommended changes in his personal behavior—*changes that in no way would have dimin-*

ished his chances of succeeding in the business world—Steve Johnson could have dramatically increased his chances of living to full life expectancy, free from many of the medical problems that prematurely dull, cripple, and kill so many Americans.

Which brings me to you—who can still do something about your life. You don't have to go the way of a Steve Johnson. Nobody, of course, can live forever; but medical science has given us new insights to greatly increase our chances for living full, alert, healthy lives. I will share those insights with you. I can show you "how to succeed in business without really dying"—but the effectiveness of what I have to say will depend on *you* and your willingness to implement the recommendations of medical science in your own life. As you read further, keep in mind what Dr. John Knowles, president of the Rockefeller Foundation, has said: "The next major advance in the health of the American people will result only from what the individual is willing to do for himself."[1]

DOING BATTLE WITH EXCESSIVE STRESS

To help you help yourself toward better health, mental alertness, and longevity, medical science has identified many of the factors that can raise havoc with a person's well-being. None seems so culpable and widespread as *stress*. It has been called the disease of our time—the scourge of modern civilizations.

Just what is stress? It is a condition we all experience. It can be caused by many things, such as frustrations, time binds, overwork, frightening experiences, emotional conflicts, and even pleasant events like marriage or an outstanding personal achievement.

Please understand that normal amounts of stress never hurt anybody; in fact, moderate amounts of stress can actually enhance performance and make for a more meaningful, exciting life. Stress becomes dangerous only when it becomes *excessive*—forcing the body to run like a car with the accelerator stuck to the floor. When we become stressed, our bodies shift into a state of high physical arousal preparing us for the so-called "fight-or-flight" response. If we experi-

---

[1]From B. Kramer, "Wiser Way of Living, Not Dramatic 'Cures,' Seen as Key to Health," *The Wall Street Journal*, Mar. 22, 1976, p. 1.

ence this state too often, or stay in it too long, we will eventually break down like any overworked machine.

The word "stress" was borrowed from the language of physics and engineering, where it refers to a "force that tends to deform a body." How apt! For that is exactly what excessive stress does to the human body in ugly, crippling ways. To compile a list of stress-related diseases is like thumbing through a medical dictionary. High blood pressure, heart attack, strokes, headaches, ulcers, allergies, infections, insomnia, asthma, diabetes, cancer, even accidents—all can be triggered and made more severe by excessive stress.

How do you know if you are under stress? One way is to visit your doctor for various tests—blood pressure, hormone levels, brain activity, and so forth. This is the preferred method, but it is not always possible on a day-to-day basis. But, as Dr. Hans Selye, an international authority on stress, points out:

> There are other indices that anyone can judge. No two people react the same way, but the usual responses are . . . you will become more irritable and will sometimes suffer insomnia, even long after the stressor agent is gone. You will usually become less capable of concentrating, and you will have an increased desire to move about. I was talking with a businessman this morning who asked if he could walk back and forth because he couldn't think well sitting down. That is a stress symptom everyone will know.[2]

Dr. Selye also points out that an increase in pulse rate and an increased tendency to sweat is common in persons undergoing stress.

DEVELOPING THE PROPER PSYCHOLOGICAL ATTITUDE TOWARD EXCESSIVE STRESS

Knowing when you are stressed is important—but it's only half the battle. It is also necessary to *do* something about it, and it is here the typical manager confronts awesome difficulties. Most supervisors readily admit they experience stress on the job. One business manager put it bluntly: "Stress is as much a part of corporate life as the annual meeting and the balance sheet." Yet many managers are hesitant to—even refuse to—reduce excessive job stress in their own lives.

[2]H. Selye (interview), "Secret of Coping with Stress," *U.S. News & World Report,* Mar. 21, 1977, p. 52.

Victimized by the stressful world they have helped create, they accept stress as a necessary component of their existence. They accept constant business stress as "immutable," a force beyond the scope of change. Then there are those who go so far as to extol the virtues of excessive stress, like the executive who, informed he had an ulcer, bragged, "I'm not concerned about it . . . don't you know that only successful people get ulcers." It is these managers, who see their stress-related miseries as "red badges of courage," proof of their business worth, who are most unwilling to do anything about excessive stress in their life. No wonder. They believe that being good in business and excessive stress go hand in hand. Unfortunately, they are wrong, and unless they change their attitude and their behavior, they may end up *dead* wrong.

To put it bluntly, there is no room for excessive stress in the American workplace. If you want to succeed in business without really dying, your main hope lies in keeping your own stress under control. I'll present the techniques to help you do this. But no techniques, however powerful, will work unless you have the proper psychological attitude toward stress in the first place. Thus, if you want to conquer excessive stress, you first must fully believe in these three statements:

1   Excessive stress does *not* have to be an immutable force in your life. It can be overcome, and I'll show you how.
2   The quickest way to succumb to an enemy is to underestimate its strength. Learn to respect stress as a formidable opponent; realize what excessive stress can do to you and decide you want to do something about it. Remember this statement: "Stress may be the corporate executive's single most powerful and pervasive enemy."[3]
3   Realize that excessive stress does *not* improve business performance. To the contrary, it has been shown to mentally and physically debilitate the manager—causing lapses in judgment, unnecessary effort, loss of concentration, reduction of creativity, interpersonal difficulties, and, in severe cases, nervous breakdowns, disease, and even death. You will *want* to overcome the "stress oppressor" when you find that it dulls rather than sharpens your managerial acuity.

Now you've taken the first big step. You realize that excessive

---

[3]"Can You Cope with Stress?" *Dun's Review*, November 1975, p. 89.

stress isn't good for you and you want to do something about it. Good. Thus you're in the proper frame of mind to launch your own stress-reduction campaign and I'm going to give you a few stress-fighting "weapons" for your arsenal. These weapons, or stress-fighting techniques, can be used alone or in combination; but remember that each one, used conscientiously, can help turn the tide in your struggle against excessive stress. Try out the various weapons and choose the best one(s) for you.

The Relaxation Response[4]

The first weapon, or technique, seems so simple that many managers dismiss it out of hand. Don't let its simplicity fool you—it works, and it works well. Furthermore, it is a weapon against stress which *all* of us possess—an innate gladiator waiting to do battle with excessive stress *at our command.*

In the words of Harvard physician Herbert Benson: "Each of us possesses a natural and innate protective mechanism against 'overstress,' which allows us to turn off harmful bodily effects, to counter the effects of the fight-or-flight response."[5] The name Dr. Benson has attached to this protective mechanism is the "relaxation response," and by using it he believes we can reduce the risk of stress-related illnesses such as heart attacks and related conditions—diseases that will cause the deaths of over 50 percent of the present population of the United States.

Just what is the relaxation response? Basically, it is a form of meditation. In calling forth the relaxation response, the meditator strives to achieve a state of "restful alertness" by spending two 20-minute periods each day in "comfortable isolation," letting the mind empty of all thoughts and distractions.

By employing the relaxation response, a person reaps many physiological benefits: decreased oxygen consumption, diminishing heart rate, lower respiratory rate, and increasing skin resistance, which is inversely related to stress. The relaxation response has also been found to increase overall memory, reduce anxiety, decrease blood pressure in hypertensive individuals, heighten perceptual ability, relieve asthma, and even alleviate dependence on certain drugs, alcohol, and tobacco.

[4]Adapted from pp. 112–113 and 114–115 in *The Relaxation Response* by Herbert Benson, M.D., with Miriam Z. Klipper. Copyright © 1975 by William Morrow and Company, Inc. By permission of the publishers.
[5]H. Benson, *The Relaxation Response,* Avon, New York, 1976, p. 25.

A real elixir, this relaxation response! Your body's natural defense against the stress spiral. Yet, as healthful as this technique is, many hardnosed managers will shun it because, as a form of meditation, they see it as "faddish hocus-pocus." Well, here is the good news. You don't need a guru, long flowing robe, or a mountaintop to practice the relaxation response. You don't even need a special "mantra" given to you in some secret ceremony. All you need is 40 minutes a day and the willingness to follow the instructions of Dr. Benson.

First, says Dr. Benson, you will need to find a *quiet, calm environment* with as few distractions as possible. Sound, even background noise, may prevent elicitation of the response. Choose a convenient, suitable place—for example, at an office desk in a quiet room or a silent area of the house.

Second, you must choose a *mental device* to focus on—for example, a single-syllable sound or word. This sound or word is repeated silently or in a low, gentle tone. The purpose of the repetition is to free oneself from logical, externally oriented thought by focusing solely on the sound or word, as repetition helps break the train of distracting thoughts. Many different words and sounds have been used in traditional practice. Because of its simplicity and neutrality, the one-syllable word "one" is suggested.

Third, you must maintain a *passive attitude*. This is very important. The purpose of the relaxation response is to help one rest and relax, and this requires a completely passive attitude. When distracting thoughts occur, they are to be disregarded and attention redirected to the single-syllable sound or word. You should not worry about how well you are performing the technique, because this may well prevent the relaxation response from occurring. Do not try to force the response, adopt a let-it-happen attitude.

Fourth, you must meditate in a *comfortable position* (comfortable for *you*). You should sit in a comfortable chair in as restful a position as possible. Your goal is to reduce any undue muscular tension. The head may be supported; the arms should be balanced or supported as well. The shoes may be removed and the feet propped up several inches, if desired. Loosen all tight-fitting clothes before beginning.[6]

Observing these four guidelines of Dr. Benson, you should be able to elicit your own relaxation response. Here is the way Dr. Benson suggests you actually conduct a session:

[6]H. Benson, "Your Innate Asset for Combating Stress," *Harvard Business Review,* July–August 1974, p. 54.

1 Sit quietly in a comfortable position.

2 Close your eyes.

3 Deeply relax all your muscles, beginning at your feet and progressing up to your face. Keep them relaxed.

4 Breathe through your nose (or mouth, if this is more comfortable). Become aware of your breathing. As you breathe out, say "One" silently to yourself. For example, breathe in . . . out, "One"; in . . . out, "One"; and so forth. Breathe easily and naturally.

5 Continue this practice for 20 minutes. You may open your eyes to check the time, but do not use an alarm. When you finish, sit quietly for several minutes, at first with your eyes closed and later with your eyes open. Do not stand up for a few minutes.

6 Remember not to worry about whether you are successful in achieving a deep level of relaxation. Maintain a passive attitude and permit relaxation to occur at its own pace. When distracting thoughts occur, try to ignore them by not dwelling upon them and return to repeating "One." With practice the response should come with little effort. Practice the technique once or twice daily, but not within 2 hours after any meal, since the digestive processes seem to interfere with elicitation of the relaxation response.[7]

There you have it. Your own innate weapon in the war on excessive stress. Use it wisely, and an equilibrium between tension and relaxation can be attained. "But," some of you may be worrying, "might the relaxation response upset my work effectiveness and make me a zombie?"

To the contrary, the relaxation response will not only combat excessive stress but will also enhance your alertness and job performance. Testimonials to that are rife in the business community. William Milton, general manager of Sprague Electric Company, refers to meditation as a "real battery charger"; Pamela Grant, director of a British printing machinery firm, says it helped her "concentrate properly for the first time in my life"; and J. Paul Chambers, president of First American Life Insurance Company claims it "helps me accomplish more with less work and effort." Dozens of American corporations, recognizing the value of the relaxation response, have initiated meditation programs at work—an idea Dr. Benson highly supports. He thinks employees should be given relaxation-response breaks instead of coffee breaks.

[7]Ibid.

The next time you want to make a really great investment in 20 minutes, why don't you take a relaxation-response break? As you do, remember the words of psychologist Daniel Goleman: "Meditators become more relaxed the longer they have been at it. At the same time they become more alert, something other ways to relax fail to bring about because they do not train the ability to pay attention. The combination of relaxation and concentration allows us to do better at whatever we try."[8]

Effective Exercise

When I ask you to practice the relaxation response, do not think I am recommending a less energetic existence—only a less stressful one. As a matter of fact, one of the best ways to beat the excessive stress syndrome is to live an active life, and our second stress-fighting weapon, exercise, will help you do just that.

"I don't know of a person who is highly regarded in medicine today who doesn't advocate exercise as an essential part of the lifestyle for healthful living."[9] So observed C. Carson Conrad while executive director of the President's Council on Physical Fitness. If you are willing to undertake an effective exercise program, you will most likely find it the *single most important* contribution you can make to your job performance and good health.

The key word here is "effective." To explain what I mean by effective, it is necessary to distinguish between two forms of exercise. One form, called aerobics, involves *sustained* activities that stimulate heart and lungs long enough to produce beneficial changes in the body. Such activities typically include walking (briskly), jogging, swimming, cycling and skipping rope. A second form of exercise does *not* require sustained action and includes sports like bowling and baseball, plus body-building activities such as weight lifting and isometrics. These undertakings can be fun, and some can give you an attractive physique, but they will *not* produce the health benefits of aerobic exercises. As science writer C. P. Gilmore notes:

> Sports such as tennis and touch football may be strenuous but they generally call for intermittent rather than prolonged effort. Golf may be

[8]D. Goleman, "Meditation Helps Break the Stress Spiral," *Psychology Today,* February 1976, p. 93.
[9]From P. Stephano, "Fitness, Health, and the National Pulse," *Action,* no. 1, 1976, p. 6.

pleasant but it does not raise the pulse rate. Calisthenics make the muscles stronger and more flexible and help keep the joints limber, but are not usually indulged in vigorously enough or long enough. And, of course, the machines that jiggle and bounce the flesh may be fun, but they do nothing for the heart.[10]

To put it bluntly, if you want to reap the health benefits from exercise, then you must be prepared to "get into" aerobics on a regular basis. This means that 4 to 6 days a week you will be expected to spend part of your time undertaking sustained, brisk physical activity. Dr. Kenneth Cooper, a noted authority on exercise and author of the informative book *The New Aerobics,* points out that you can achieve total aerobic fitness by running 1½ miles in from 12 to just under 15 minutes five times a week. This means you can achieve top physical fitness with a time investment of under 15 minutes a day; a little over an hour a week. As there are 1440 minutes in every day, spending 15 minutes on exercise seems like a worthwhile investment for better job performance, alertness, and health.

Of course, running that fast might not be your cup of tea. Do not despair! You can enjoy full aerobic fitness at a more leisurely pace—you'll just have to spend more time at the activity you choose. For example, instead of running the mile and a half in the 12- to 15-minute range, you may choose to walk it instead; then you will have to do so twice daily, five times a week, in 21½ minutes—which isn't exactly a marathon distance in jackrabbit time. What this means, best of all, is that the health benefits of aerobic fitness are within the reach of almost everyone—young and old. You don't need to be a young person or a "jock" to become aerobically fit—you don't even have to run. All you need is a little motivation, training, and perseverance, and you can walk your way to better health.

Just what *are* the benefits of regular, sustained, brisk exercise? One of the best ways to find out is to ask people involved in aerobics. Chances are their missionary zeal will send you scurrying for your sneakers. Most veteran exercisers agree that once you get into aerobics, you'll wonder how you ever got along without it. The benefits they (myself included) have experienced first hand are documented by scientific research.

[10]C. Gilmore, "And the Beat Goes On," *St. Petersburg Times,* Apr. 1, 1977, p. 1–D.

Would you be willing to spend some time, 4 to 6 days a week, to gain the advantages associated with lower blood pressure, substantial and permanent weight loss, healthier blood chemistry, and increased strength and efficiency of the heart? Regular aerobic exercise produces these beneficial physiological changes and more. It also helps those with diabetes and insomnia; and many doctors believe it can aid in the battle against the number one killer: heart disease. Some medical authorities question the preventive value of sustained exercise but support the notion that it can be very useful in rehabilitating heart victims. Others, like Dr. Cooper, believe that aerobics, properly followed, will lessen a person's chances of prematurely developing coronary heart disease or related vascular ailments. One physician, Dr. Thomas Bassler, goes so far as to claim that anyone in physical condition to run and finish a marathon will be permanently immune to heart attacks. Although his argument is controversial, it is interesting to note that Dr. Bassler heads a 1000-member group of running MD's called the American Medical Joggers Association. It is my belief that when doctors start "running for their lives," it might be the better part of wisdom to keep pretty close behind.

Regular aerobic exercise has also improved the psychological well-being of many participants.[11] A better self-image and more self-confidence are reported by many exercising managers, along with increased alertness and ability to concentrate. These individuals report they work with more energy and need less sleep when following an exercise regimen. A large study by the National Aeronautics and Space Administration is interesting in this respect. Among NASA employees who closely followed a fitness program, more than 90 percent reported a feeling of better health and stamina, and about 50 percent said they had a more positive work attitude with less strain and tension.

This brings us to the last major benefit of aerobic exercise. It helps reduce the manager's major enemy: excessive stress. Simply put, exercise is a kind of pressure-release valve that provides an outlet for stored-up tensions. It allows us to express our aggressive drives in physical action rather than keep them pent up inside where they can produce excessive stress effects. Also, a physically fit person's body is toned to a point where it can withstand stress more effectively. As

[11]A. Ismail and L. Trachtman, "Jogging the Imagination," *Psychology Today*, March 1973, pp. 79–82.

writers Walter McQuade and Ann Aikman have noted, "A person who is in good physical condition will withstand the assault of a virus, or a spell of overwork—or even a quarrel with the foreman—better than someone who isn't."[12]

So much for the benefits of exercise. The human body wasn't built to sit still, so it shouldn't come as a surprise to discover that aerobic exercise is good for us. Yet some of you may be worrying about the possible *dangers* of sustained exercise—you may have heard stories about joggers dying or injuring themselves. Many of these stories turn out to be greatly exaggerated; but it is true that aerobic exercise is demanding and can be potentially dangerous for people who ignore simple basic safety precautions. For those who *do* observe these precautions, sustained exercise is both safe and beneficial. In your own exercise program you should observe these rules:

1 See your doctor for a complete medical examination *before* you begin exercising. This is very important. The vast majority of managers will be able to undertake aerobic exercise with no difficulty; however, a small number of individuals might have hidden problems—like an unknown heart condition—that could make sustained exercise risky. Tell your doctor you intend to begin an aerobic program, so that he can advise you of any possible problems. Most exercise physiologists recommend that the checkup include a cardio-pulmonary stress test.

2 Start slowly and gradually work your way up to good aerobic fitness. If you've spent 30 years getting out of shape, don't expect youthful vigor to return as soon as you pull on your sweat socks. If you have any questions, Dr. Cooper's *The New Aerobics* gives detailed instructions on how you can progress safely to physical fitness and what you have to do to maintain it. Each person follows a program based on age and current physical condition.[13]

3 Exercise regularly—at least three times a week—or do not exercise at all.

4 If you experience discomfort or pain while exercising, stop and check with your physician before you exercise again.

5 Prior to exercise, it is helpful to do a few calisthenics to limber up and get your body toned for action. After finishing aerobic

[12]W. McQuade and A. Aikman, *Stress,* Bantam, New York, 1975, p. 130.
[13]K. Cooper, *The New Aerobics,* Bantam, New York, 1970.

exercise, it is recommended that you let your body readjust by doing some slow walking or a similar "warming down" activity.

6 Do not overexert yourself during exercise. A good guideline for determining if you exercise too vigorously is your pulse rate. Five minutes after you exercise it should be under 120, according to Dr. Cooper. Ten minutes after exercise it should be back to below 100. Dr. Cooper also suggests you watch for these symptoms of overexertion during exercise: "Tightness or pain in the chest, severe breathlessness, light-headedness, dizziness, loss of muscle control and nausea. Should you experience any of these symptoms," he cautions, "stop exercising immediately."[14]

There you have six rules for making your exercise program medically sound and worthwhile. Remember you are exercising to achieve better health. You defeat that purpose if you don't exercise safely.

The value of aerobic exercise for managers is becoming more evident everyday. I hope that you will consider using this weapon in your fight against excessive stress. After all, company after company is instituting aerobic exercise programs (see Box 10-1); don't you think it's time you did, too?

[14]Ibid., p. 42.

BOX 10-1

A COMPANY WITH A TRACK RECORD*

If you asked an executive of Tyler Corporation about the company's track record, you might get an answer in terms of times and distances rather than profits and loss. This is because Tyler is one of the growing number of American corporations actively supporting jogging programs as a way to assure aerobic fitness in company management.

*Material and quotes for this box were taken from an article by R. Rowan, "The Company That Just Runs and Runs," *Fortune*, Dec. 4, 1978, pp. 94–97. Other articles of interest on the same topic include: D. Norfolk, "Keeping Fit to Manage," *Management Today*, March 1976, pp. 101ff.; and K. Moore, "A Run for Their Money," *Sports Illustrated*, November 4, 1974, pp. 68ff.

> Says Tyler's chairman and president, Joseph F. McKinney: "Running, like business, is full of drudgery. But inherent in our philosophy is the belief that physical fitness gives us a headstart over a less fit competitor."
> All that running must be doing something right. In the past decade Tyler Corporation sales "have sextupled (to $365 million) and net income has increased almost nine times (to $21 million)."
> McKinney's enthusiasm for aerobic fitness has stretched beyond the boundaries of his own company. One result: the Tyler Cup race for corporation executives. And not just "small time" executives, either! In fact, in a recent race 170 executives representing ". . . seventy-two companies with a total of 1.5 million employees and $90 billion in assets" lined up in the starting blocks.

The relaxation response and aerobic exercise are two weapons *all of us* can employ in the war on excessive stress. I have two other weapons left to present, each for combating a specific difficulty that creates excessive stress. If you don't have these difficulties, then you won't have to deploy these weapons against them. I hope you'll never have to use them. Unfortunately, scientific evidence suggests that the majority of people in business are experiencing one or both of these difficulties—and should be doing something about it.

Dealing with Job Dissatisfaction

The first of these difficulties involves job dissatisfaction. As we already saw in Section 1 of this book, many workers are unhappy with their jobs—and among them are managers. According to Dr. Harry Johnson, recently retired chairman of the medical board of the Life Extension Institute, "being in the wrong job accounts for a major percentage of stress problems in executives."[15]

It is important to note that the cause of medical problems is *not* work itself but, rather, the mismatch between the worker and the work performed. Put another way, we might say that one person's job is another person's poison. In this context, I'd like to share with you the insights of Dr. Selye, the stress authority mentioned earlier in the chapter.

[15]F. Stone, "A Sound Mind . . . ," *Management Review*, January 1975, p. 7.

Dr. Selye has spent a lifetime studying the relationship between stress and work and has developed an interesting theory. Work, to him, is a basic need in all of us—it is *not* to be avoided. He claims that "to function normally, man needs work as he needs air, food, sleep, social contacts, and sex." Further, stress is associated with every kind of work—*but,* if you like your work and are successful at it, this kind of stress won't harm you. Trouble occurs when workers don't like what they are doing or see a discrepancy between their job and their goals in life. This leads to *distress,* which can cause a whole host of miseries.

Dr. Selye's message is clear as a bell. Work is not harmful; a person's not enjoying work is. By the way, at the age of 18, Selye began his study of medicine—work he dearly loved. He worked from 4 A.M. till 6 P.M. At age 67, he still loved his work and kept exactly the same hours.

Are you one of those people who enjoy their work? Do you awaken in the morning looking forward to your job? If so, you are fortunate. But if you are seriously dissatisfied with your job, then you have three alternatives. You can stay at the job—spend at least 8 hours a day being unhappy—and risk the medical dangers associated with excessive stress; or you can try to maintain your present position but alter what you do to make it more interesting and in line with your life goals; if this is not possible, you can attempt to change jobs or careers.

Obviously, changing careers is not something to be taken lightly. But, then, neither is a lifetime spent at "distressful" labor. Dr. David Fink recognizes the importance of changing directions in life. He recommends making a fresh start "if your life has led you into a detour that is taking you where you do not want to go." And he goes on to say:

> It may be tough; tomorrow it will be tougher, because you will be that much farther away from your destination. . . . To many, this advice to redirect your own life will sound somehow subversive, radical, and dangerous. Nothing could be farther from the truth. If you want to subvert your life, to undermine it radically, live it against the direction of the flow of your real personality. If your job makes you sick, quit it. What difference does it make how good it is if it isn't good for you?[16]

[16]D. Fink, *Release from Nervous Tension,* Pocket Books, New York, 1973, pp. 200–201.

No job is going to be joyous and fulfilling all the time; and the decision to make a change should not be based on petty annoyances or momentary fits of pique. There is a line between the "trials and tribulations" of management and the tragedy of unfulfilling work. If you feel you have crossed over that line, Dr. Fink suggests you take five steps:

> **1** Make a list of your talents and skills.
>
> **2** Ask yourself what kind of work would give you an opportunity to exercise those talents and skills.
>
> **3** Pick that vocation within your scope which will furnish the most satisfactions.
>
> **4** Make a decision, and get started. If you need further training, that is priority number one.
>
> **5** All of your old activities and habits that do not fit in with your new purpose are out for the duration.[17]

Our third stress-fighting weapon involves making modifications in the work you do. I realize that current realities—the job market, the problem of credentials, financial considerations—might discourage use of such a weapon. Yet, a manager should also assess the realities of an unsatisfying job—the high potential for poor health and unfulfilled needs—and weigh these against the risks of job or even career modifications.

Should you use such a weapon? Take stock of where you are, carefully analyzing your own particular circumstances, and you should be able to determine which course of action to take. One manager put it this way: "Work to your heart's content; but if your heart isn't in your work, then your heart may very well put you out of work."

Eliminating Type A Behavior

Speaking of your heart brings us to our final weapon for combating excessive stress—a weapon designed to break you out of the dangerous stress spiral and help you combat America's number one killer: heart disease. What is this weapon? A change in diet? A new drug? No. The weapon is the elimination of Type A behavior from your personality.

[17]Ibid., p. 209.

Type A is a term created by two heart specialists, Drs. Meyer Friedman and Ray Rosenman, to describe a behavior pattern they think is the *major* cause of premature coronary heart disease. They sound a very strong warning: "In the absence of Type A Behavior Pattern, coronary heart disease almost never occurs before seventy years of age. . . . But when this behavior pattern is present, coronary heart disease can easily erupt in one's thirties or forties."[18]

How many American business managers exhibit the Type A behavior? If current estimates are correct, about 50 percent of the men and a growing number of the women in managerial positions possess the deadly Type A personality. It is those individuals who must alter their behavior, according to Drs. Friedman and Rosenman, if they want to reduce their risk of heart disease.

Just what *is* Type A behavior? Some describe it as "hurry sickness." Others label it "compulsive striving." Here is how Drs. Friedman and Rosenman define it:

> . . . a style of living characterized by excesses or competitiveness, striving for achievement, aggressiveness (sometimes stringently re-pressed), time urgency, acceleration of common activities, restlessness, hostility, hyper-alertness, explosiveness of speech amplitude, tenseness of facial musculature and feelings of struggle against the limitations of time and the insensitivity of the environment. This torrent of life is usually, but not always, channeled into a vocation or profession with such dedication that Type A persons often neglect other aspects of their life, such as family and recreation.[19]

Sound familiar? I suspect so. In the business world where racing against the clock is as American as apple pie, one should not be surprised at the number of Type A personalities around. The question is, How *long* will they be around? This is what worries Drs. Friedman and Rosenman, who want business managers to develop a "Type B" personality. In most ways, the Type B behavior pattern is the exact opposite of Type A. The Type B person isn't locked in a constant struggle to "beat the clock." Such an individual can also be ambitious,

---

[18]M. Friedman and R. Rosenman, *Type A Behavior and Your Heart,* Fawcett-Crest, New York, 1974, p. 9.

[19]Quoted in J. Howard, P. Rechnitzer, and D. Cunningham, "Coping with Job Tension—Effective and Ineffective Methods," *Public Personnel Management,* September–October, 1975, p. 318.

but feels more confident and secure than the Type A person and is able to be more relaxed. Most important, Type B persons are just as successful as their Type A counterparts; they just handle themselves differently. They also live long enough to enjoy the fruits of their labor.

To help determine what kind of personality *you* have—Type A or Type B—Drs. Friedman and Rosenman developed a Type A self-identification test. An adapted version is included in Box 10-2. Take a moment to read the instructions carefully; then take the test.

BOX 10-2

TYPE A SELF-IDENTIFICATION TEST*

INSTRUCTIONS

Here is a test to help you determine whether you are a Type A or Type B personality. If you are honest in your self-appraisal . . . we believe you will not have too much trouble accomplishing this. . . . Incidentally, we have found that Type A persons are by and large more common, and that if you are not quite sure about yourself, chances are that you, too, are Type A—not fully developed, perhaps, but bad enough to think about changing. And after you have assessed yourself, ask a friend or your spouse whether your self-assessment was accurate. If you disagree, *they* are probably right.

YOU POSSESS TYPE A BEHAVIOR PATTERN

   1 If you have (a) a habit of explosively accentuating various key words in your ordinary speech even when there is no real need for such accentuation, and (b) a tendency to utter the last few words of your sentences far more rapidly than the opening words.

   2 If you *always* move, walk, and eat rapidly.

   3 If you feel (particularly if you openly exhibit to others) an impatience with the rate at which most events take place. Here are some examples of this sort of impatience: if you become *unduly* irritated or even enraged when a car ahead of you in your lane runs at a pace you consider too slow; if you find it anguishing to wait in a line or to wait your turn to be seated at a restaurant; if you find it intolerable

   *Adapted from M. Friedman & R. Rosenman, *Type A Behavior and Your Heart,* Knopf, New York, 1974.

---

to watch others perform tasks you know you can do faster; if you find it difficult to restrain yourself from hurrying the speech of others.

4 If you indulge in *polyphasic* thought or performance, frequently striving to think of or do two or more things simultaneously. Some examples: while trying to listen to another person's speech you persist in continuing to think about an irrelevant subject; while golfing or fishing you continue to ponder your business or professional problems; while using an electric razor you attempt also to eat your breakfast or drive your car; or while driving your car you attempt to dictate letters for your secretary. This is one of the commonest traits in the Type A person.

5 If you find it *always* difficult to refrain from talking about or bringing the theme of any conversation around to those subjects which especially interest and intrigue you, and when unable to accomplish this maneuver, you pretend to listen but really remain preoccupied with your own thoughts.

6 If you almost always feel vaguely guilty when you relax and do absolutely nothing for several hours to several days.

7 If you no longer observe the more important or interesting or lovely objects that you encounter in your milieu. For example, if you enter a strange office, store, or home, and after leaving any of these places you cannot recall what was in them, you no longer are observing well—or for that matter enjoying life very much.

8 If you do not have any time to spare to become the things worth *being* because you are so preoccupied with getting the things worth *having*.

9 If you attempt to schedule more and more in less and less time, and in doing so make fewer and fewer allowances for unforeseen contingencies. A concomitant of this is a *chronic sense of time urgency*, one of the core components of the Type A behavior pattern.

10 If on meeting another severely afflicted Type A person, instead of feeling compassion for his affliction, you find yourself compelled to "challenge" him. This is a telltale trait because no one arouses the aggressive and/or hostile feelings of one Type A subject more quickly than another Type A subject.

11 If you resort to certain characteristic gestures or nervous tics. For example, if in conversation you frequently clench your fist, or bang your hand upon a table, or pound one fist into the palm of your other hand in order to emphasize a conversational point, you are exhibiting Type A gestures. Similarly, if the corners of your mouth spasmodically, in ticlike fashion, jerk backward slightly exposing your teeth, or if you habitually clench your jaw, or even grind your teeth, you are subject to muscular phenomena suggesting the presence of a continuous *struggle,* which is, of course, the kernel of the Type A behavior pattern.

12   If you believe that whatever success you have enjoyed has been due in good part to your ability to get things done faster than other people, and if you are afraid to stop doing everything faster and faster.

13   If you find yourself increasingly and ineluctably committed to translating and evaluating not only your own but also the activities of others in terms of numbers.

YOU POSSESS THE TYPE B BEHAVIOR PATTERN

1   If you are completely free of *all* the habits and exhibit none of the traits we have listed that harass the severely afflicted Type A person.

2   If you never suffer from a sense of time urgency with its accompanying impatience.

3   If you harbor no free-floating hostility, and you feel no need to display or discuss either your achievements or accomplishments unless such exposure is demanded by the situation.

4   If when you play, you do so to find fun and relaxation, not to exhibit your superiority at any cost.

5   If you can relax without guilt, just as you can work without agitation.

How did you do? Of course, nobody is a pure Type A or Type B person—but, in general, which behavior pattern seems to fit you best? If you possess many of the characteristics of the Type A personality, you should take steps *now* to try and do something about it. As Drs. Friedman and Rosenman point out, ". . . in the majority of cases, Type A Behavior Patterns can be altered and altered drastically; and it is a terribly dangerous delusion to believe otherwise."[20]

Regretfully, there is no simple formula that can transform you from a Type A into a Type B personality overnight. Changing behavior

[20]Friedman and Rosenman, op. cit., p. 209.

patterns, particularly ones as socially acceptable and deeply ingrained as Type A behavior patterns, will take a lot of time and conscientious effort. In extreme cases, moving away from destructive Type A behavior will require significant changes in your basic lifestyle. But the changes *can* be made, and they *will* be worth it. To help you, Drs. Friedman and Rosenman offer some good suggestions. Here are a few of them, along with some of my own.

1 Realize that you can be just as successful in business by being Type B as by being Type A. Drs. Friedman and Rosenman see Type A behavior as actually detrimental to long-term success, and they tell Type A business people: "If you have been successful, it is not *because* of your Type A Behavior Pattern, but *despite* it."

2 Do not think you'll be lucky enough to escape the medical consequences of long-term Type A behavior. Many Type A persons delude themselves in such a manner, and therefore don't try to modify their potentially dangerous actions.

3 During each day, set some time aside for rest and relaxation.

4 Allow yourself enough time to get things done, so that you won't have to feel pressured and rushed. For example, leave ample time between your appointments.

5 Quit trying to think of or do more than one thing at a time. Concentrate on one task at a time.

6 Live by the calendar, not the stopwatch.

7 Learn to take breaks when doing work that can cause you stress.

8 Try to work in a setting that promotes peace of mind. Constant interruptions, messy desks, and drab surroundings do not help soothe the ragged mind.

9 Remind yourself once a day that no enterprise ever failed because it was executed too slowly, too well.

10 Acquire a taste for reading.

11 Spend some time with just yourself.

12 When facing a task, ask yourself two questions: Will this matter be important 5 years from now? Must I do this right now, or do I have enough time to think about the *best* way to accomplish it?

13 Don't think you have to finish all your work by 5 P.M. every day. The world will still be around when you wake up the next morning.

14 Avoid irritating, overcompetitive people.

15 Learn to slow down and be patient with the rate at which events take place. When you act rushed, you will feel pressured. Eat slower; walk slower; don't drive as if you were in the Indianapolis 500; try to talk slower; quit rushing the conversation of others; learn to wait in line without getting the jitters.[21]

I hope you will find these suggestions helpful in battling Type A behavior in your life. Drs. Friedman and Rosenman recommend these and others in their book if you would like further methods for combating the Type A syndrome. The two doctors also emphasize that it's never too late to begin a Type A prevention program—even if you're in your sixties and a victim of one or more heart attacks. One MD began just such a program after a heart attack in 1967. His name is Meyer Friedman.

The Bottom Line

Heart attacks, excessive stress, relaxation, exercise—I've deluged you with a lot of information; tendered some suggestions; sounded some warnings; and, I hope, sparked your enthusiasm for practicing preventive medicine in your own life.

Social historians tell us we are living in an age of ecology. We speak of the need to reduce waste, to save precious resources. Do you know of any greater waste than the needless waste of human life? Do you know of any resource more precious than the human resource? Practice a little personal ecology: take the steps necessary to enhance your chances for living a healthier, happier, and more active and productive life. You *can* succeed in business without really dying. Make it your business to do so.

[21]Ibid., pp. 207–271.

BIBLIOGRAPHY

Andrews, L., and M. Karlins: *Requiem for Democracy?*, Holt, New York; 1971.

"Are You a Candidate for Heart Disease?" *Supervisory Management*, October 1974, pp. 39–42.

Beatty, R., and C. Schneier: "A Case for Positive Reinforcement," *Business Horizons*, April 1975, pp. 57–66.

Benson, H.: "Your Innate Asset for Combating Stress," *Harvard Business Review*, July-August 1974, pp. 49–60.

————: *The Relaxation Response*, Avon, New York, 1976.

"Big Firms Start to Talk Job Enrichment," *Industry Week*, July 9, 1973, pp. 42–46.

Boxx, W., and J. Chambless: "Preventive Health Maintenance for Executives," *California Management Review*, Fall 1975, pp. 49–54.

Cangemi, J., and J. Claypool: "Complimentary Interviews: A System for Rewarding Outstanding Employees," *Personnel Journal*, February 1978, pp. 87–90.

"Can You Cope with Stress?" *Dun's Review*, November 1975, pp. 89–90.

Cecil-Wright, J.: "How to Use Incentives," *Management Today*, January 1978, pp. 76ff.

Clutterbuck, D.: "Motivation Programme Is a Give-Away," *International Management*, August 1977, pp. 40–41.

"Commuter Stress," *Science Digest*, August 1975, pp. 18–19.

Cooper, K.: *The New Aerobics*, M. Evans, New York; 1970; paperback ed., Bantam, New York, 1970.

"Coping with Stress," *Industrial Management*, November 1975, pp. 32–36.

"Cracking under Stress," *U.S. News & World Report*, May 10, 1976, pp. 59–61.

Curley, D.: "Employee Sounding Boards: Answering the Participative Need," *Personnel Administrator*, May 1978, pp. 69ff.

"Deep Sensing: A Pipeline to Employee Morale," *Business Week*, Jan. 29, 1979, pp. 124ff.

Donnelly, J.: "Participative Management at Work," *Harvard Business Review*, January-February 1977, pp. 117–127.

Dowling, W.: "At General Motors: System 4 Builds Performance and Profits," *Organizational Dynamics*, Winter 1975, pp. 23–38.

Dreyfack, R.: "Dismal Disincentives," *Management Review*, December 1976, pp. 48–51.

Dutton, R.: "The Executive and Physical Fitness," *Personnel Administration*, March-April 1966, pp. 13–18.

Dyson, B.: "Leading to Satisfaction," *Management Today*, April 1975, pp. 76ff.

"Executive's Guide to Living with Stress," *Business Week,* Aug. 23, 1976, pp. 75–80.

Field, R.: "Scorecard for Heart Attacks," *Science Digest,* May 1976, pp. 87–88.

"Fighting Stress," *Dun's Review,* January 1977, pp. 59–61.

Fink, D.: *Release from Nervous Tension,* Pocket Books, New York, 1973.

"Flying High on an Idea," *Nation's Business,* August 1978, pp. 41–48 (interview with M. Ash).

Friedman, M., and R. Rosenman: *Type A Behavior and Your Heart,* Fawcett-Crest Books, New York, 1974.

Friis, R.: "Job Dissatisfaction and Coronary Heart Disease," *Intellect,* May-June 1976, pp. 594–596.

Galambos, A.: "There Is an Alternative to 'Shape Up or Ship Out'!" *Supervisory Management,* November 1977, pp. 16–21.

Giblin, E.: "Motivating Employees: A Closer Look," *Personnel Journal,* February 1976, pp. 68–72.

Gilmore, C.: "And the Beat Goes On," *St. Petersburg Times,* Apr. 1, 1977, p. 1-D.

———: "Does Exercise Really Prolong Life?" *Reader's Digest,* July 1977, pp. 140–143.

Glass, D.: "Stress, Competition and Heart Attacks," *Psychology Today,* December 1976, pp. 54ff.

Goleman, D.: "Meditation Helps Break the Stress Spiral," *Psychology Today,* February 1976, pp. 82ff.

Gullett, R., and R. Reisen: "Behavior Modification: A Contingency Approach to Employee Performance," *Personnel Journal,* April 1975, pp. 206–211.

Hekimian, J., and C. Jones: "Put People on Your Balance Sheet," *Harvard Business Review,* January-February 1967, pp. 105ff.

Homans, G.: "The Western Electric Researches," in S. Hoslett (ed.), *Human Factors in Management,* Harper, New York, 1951.

"How to Survive in Business," *Newsweek,* July 14, 1975, p. 64.

Howard, J., P. Rechnitzer, and D. Cunningham: "Coping with Job Tension—Effective and Ineffective Methods," *Public Personnel Management,* September-October 1975, pp. 317–326.

Huebner, H., and A. Johnson: "Behavior Modification: An Aid in Solving Personnel Problems," *Personnel Administrator,* October 1974, pp. 31–34.

Ismail, A., and L. Trachtman: "Jogging the Imagination," *Psychology Today,* March 1973, pp. 79–82.

Janis, I., D. Kaye, and P. Kirschner: "Facilitating Effects of 'Eating-While-Reading' on Responsiveness to Persuasive Communications," *Journal of Personality and Social Psychology,* vol. 1, 1965, pp. 181–186.

Jenkins, D.: "Democracy in the Factory," *The Atlantic,* April 1973, pp. 78–83.

Jewett, M.: "Employee Benefits: The Need to Know," *Personnel Journal,* January 1976, pp. 18–22.

Kafka, V., and J. Schaefer: "What's Your Motivational Rating?" *Training and Development Journal,* October 1977, pp. 38–40.

Kane M.: "Scorecard," *Sports Illustrated,* July 24, 1972, pp. 6–7.

Karlins, M., and H. Abelson: *Persuasion,* Springer, New York, 1970.

———— and L. Andrews: *Biofeedback,* Lippincott, New York, 1972.

———— and ————: *Psychology: What's In It for Us?"* Random House, New York, 1973.

Kenton, L.: "Management's Toughest Course," *Industrial Management,* November 1976, pp. 10–14.

Kirby, P.: "Productivity Increases through Feedback Systems," *Personnel Journal,* October 1977, pp. 512–515.

Kotulak, R.: "Stress: A Small Reward of the Good Life," *Miami Herald,* June 1, 1976, Sec. F.

Kovach, K.: "Improving Employee Motivation in Today's Business Environment," *MSU Business Topics,* Autumn 1976, pp. 5–12.

Kramer, B.: "Wiser Way of Living, Not Dramatic 'Cures,' Seen as Key to Health," *The Wall Street Journal,* Mar. 22, 1976, p. 1.

Kreitner, R.: "People Are Systems, Too: Filling the Feedback Vacuum," *Business Horizons,* November 1977, pp. 54–58.

Lamott, K.: "What to Do When Stress Signs Say You're Killing Yourself," *Today's Health,* January 1975, pp. 30ff.

Lawler, E.: "Workers Can Set Their Own Wages Responsibly," *Psychology Today,* February 1977, pp. 109ff.

————: "Developing a Motivating Work Climate," *Management Review,* July 1977, pp. 25ff.

Lazer, R.: "Behavior Modification as a Managerial Technique," *The Conference Board Record,* January 1975, pp. 22–25.

Leavitt, H.: *Managerial Psychology,* rev. ed., University of Chicago Press, Chicago, 1964.

Loving, R.: "W. T. Grant's Last Days—as Seen from Store 1192," *Fortune,* April 1976, pp. 126–130.

Maccoby, M.: "The Corporate Climber," *Fortune,* December 1976, pp. 98–108.

McQuade, W., and A. Aikman: *Stress,* Bantam, New York, 1975.

Markin, R., and C. Lillis: "Sales Managers Get What They Expect," *Business Horizons,* June 1975, pp. 51–58.

Martin, R.: "Five Principles of Corrective Disciplinary Action," *Supervisory Management,* January 1978, pp. 24ff.

Maslow, A.: *Motivation and Personality,* Harper, New York, 1954.

Mayer, A., and M. Ruby: "One Firm's Family," *Newsweek,* Nov. 21, 1977, pp. 82–88.

Mayo, E., F. Roethlisberger, and W. Dickson: *Management and the Worker,* Harvard, Cambridge, Mass.; 1939.

Mayr, O.: "The Origins of Feedback Control," *Scientific American,* no. 223, 1970, pp. 110–118.

Mealiea, L.: "The TA Approach to Employee Development," *Supervisory Management,* August 1977, pp. 11–19.

Mee, J. (interview): "Understanding the Attitudes of Today's Employees," *Nation's Business,* August 1976, pp. 22–28.

Meyer, P.: "If Hitler Asked You to Electrocute a Stranger, Would You? Probably," *Esquire,* February 1970, pp. 130ff.

Milgram, S.: "Behavioral Study of Obedience," *Journal of Abnormal and Social Psychology,* vol. 67, 1963, pp. 371–378.

————: "Some Conditions of Obedience and Disobedience to Authority," *Human Relations,* vol. 18, 1965, pp. 57–76.

Moore, K.: "A Run for Their Money," *Sports Illustrated,* Nov. 4, 1974, pp. 68–78.

Moore, L.: "Motivation through Positive Reinforcement," *Supervisory Management,* October 1976, pp. 2–9.

"New Tool: Reinforcement for Good Work," *Psychology Today,* April 1972, pp. 67–69.

Norfolk, D.: "Keeping Fit to Manage," *Management Today,* March 1976, pp. 101–103.

Northrup, B.: "Working Happier . . . ," *The Wall Street Journal,* Oct. 25, 1974, pp. 1ff.

Oberle, R.: "Administering Disciplinary Actions," *Personnel Journal,* January 1978, pp. 29–31.

Page, R.: *How to Lick Executive Stress,* Prentice-Hall, Englewood Cliffs, N.J., 1977.

"Participative Management, Bonuses Boost Productivity for Michigan Firm," *Commerce Today,* Nov. 11, 1974, pp. 12–13.

Pascarella, P.: "What Makes a Good Manager?" *Industry Week,* Sept. 1, 1975, pp. 33–42.

Piers, P., *Alive,* Lippincott, New York, 1974.

"Productivity Gains from a Pat on the Back," *Business Week,* Jan. 23, 1978, pp. 56ff.

"Quality of Work Life," *The Wall Street Journal,* Feb. 3, 1976, p. 1.

Rabkin, J., and E. Struening: "Life Events, Stress, and Illness," *Science,* Dec. 3, 1976, pp. 1013–1020.

"Recognizing Merit at Xerox," *Management Review,* June 1978, p. 44.

Repp, W.: "Motivating the NOW Generation," *Personnel Journal,* July 1971, pp. 540ff.

Roach, J.: "Managing Psychological Man," *Management Review,* June 1977, pp. 27ff.

Robins, J.: "Firms Try Newer Way to Slash Absenteeism as Carrot and Stick Fail . . . ," *The Wall Street Journal,* Mar. 14, 1979, pp. 1ff.

Rosenbaum, B.: "Understanding and Using Motivation," *Supervisory Management,* January 1979, pp. 9–13.

Rosow, J.: "Solving the Human Equation in the Productivity Puzzle," *Management Review,* August 1977, pp. 40–43.

Rossiter, A.: "Cholesterol from Jogging Seems to Be Good for You, New Research Indicates," *St. Petersburg Times,* Jan. 28, 1977, pp. 2-Dff.

Rotondi, T.: "Behavior Modification on the Job," *Supervisory Management,* February 1976, pp. 23–28.

Rowan, R.: "The Company That Runs and Runs," *Fortune,* Dec. 4, 1978, pp. 94–97.

Salpukas, A.: "Work Democracy Tested at Scandinavian Plants," *The New York Times,* Nov. 11, 1974.

———: "Swedish Auto Plant Drops Assembly Line," *The New York Times,* Nov. 12, 1974.

———: "Plant is Experimenting with Changing Work on Line," *The New York Times,* Apr. 9, 1975, p. 24.

Sawyer, K.: "Work Habits in U.S. Changing," *St. Petersburg Times,* Jan. 1, 1978, pp. 1ff.

Schrank, R.: "How to Relieve Worker Boredom," *Psychology Today,* July 1978, pp. 79–80.

Schroder, H., M. Karlins, and J. Phares: *Education for Freedom,* Wiley, New York, 1973.

Scott, E.: "Motivation, Productivity and the American Worker," unpublished manuscript, 1978.

Selye, H.: *Stress Without Distress,* Lippincott, New York, 1974.

——— (interview): "Secret of Coping with Stress," *U.S. News & World Report,* Mar. 21, 1977, pp. 51–53.

Shelton, B.: "'Team Spirit' Results in Higher Productivity, Job Satisfaction," *Commerce Today,* Sept. 30, 1974, pp. 5–6.

Sherif, M., and C Sherif: *Social Psychology,* Harper, New York, 1969.

Skinner, B.: *Walden Two,* Macmillan, New York, 1948.

Spiegel, D.: "How Not to Motivate," *Supervisory Management,* November 1977, pp. 11–15.

Steinbrink, J.: "How to Pay Your Sales Force," *Harvard Business Review,* July-August 1978, pp. 94–122.

Stephano, P.: "Fitness, Health, and the National Pulse," *Action,* no. 1, 1976, pp. 6–7.

Stone, F.: "A Sound Mind . . . ," *Management Review,* January 1975, pp. 4–11.

Student, K.: "Changing Values and Management Stress," *Personnel,* January–February 1977, pp. 48–55.

"Stunning Turnaround at Tarrytown," *Time,* May 5, 1980, p. 87.

Suinn, R.: "How to Break the Vicious Cycle of Stress," *Psychology Today,* December 1976, pp. 59ff.

Swengros, G. (interview): ". . . A Sound Body," *Management Review,* January 1975, pp. 12–21.

Tarkenton, F.: "Productivity and Job Satisfaction," *American Express Newsletter,* April 1980, pp. 1ff.

"'Team Spirit' Results in Higher Productivity, Job Satisfaction," *Commerce Today,* Sept. 30, 1974, pp. 5–6.

"The Growing Disaffection with 'Workaholism,'" *Business Week,* Feb. 27, 1978, p. 97.

Townsend, R.: *Up the Organization,* Fawcett-Crest, New York, 1970.

Truell, G.: "Core Managerial Strategies Culled from Behavioral Research," *Supervisory Management,* January 1977, pp. 10–17.

Twain, M.: *The Adventures of Tom Sawyer,* Heritage Press, New York, 1936.

Velghe, J., and G. Cockrell: "What Makes Johnny Mop?" *Personnel Journal,* June 1975, pp. 324ff.

Walsh, R.: "You Can Deal with Stress," *Supervisory Management,* October 1975, pp. 16–21.

Watson, J.: *Behaviorism,* People's Institute, New York, 1924.

—— and R. Rayner: "Conditioned Emotional Reactions," *Journal of Experimental Psychology,* 3, 1920, 1–14.

Ways, M.: "The American Kind of Worker Participation," *Fortune,* October 1976, pp. 168–182.

Whitehill, A.: "Maintenance Factors: The Neglected Side of Worker Motivation," *Personnel Journal,* October 1976, pp. 516–526.

Whyte, W.: *Money and Motivation,* Harper, New York, 1955.

Wilbur, L.: "But Do You Inspire Your Employees? *Supervision,* November 1976, pp. 4–5.

Witkin, A. (interview): "How Bosses Get People to Work Harder," *U.S. News & World Report,* Jan. 29, 1979, pp. 63–64.

Index